Take a Hike!

Family Walks in the Finger Lakes
and Genesee Valley Region

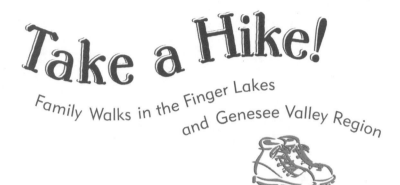

Take a Hike!

Family Walks in the Finger Lakes and Genesee Valley Region

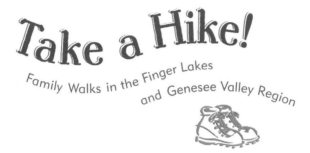

By Rich & Sue Freeman

Footprint Press
Fishers, New York 14453
http://www.footprintpress.com

Other books available from Footprint Press:

Take A Hike! Family Walks in the Rochester Area
Take Your Bike! Family Rides in the Rochester Area
Take Your Bike! Family Rides in the Finger Lakes
  & Genesee Valley Region
Bruce Trail – An Adventure Along the Niagara Escarpment
Alter – A Simple Path to Emotional Wellness

Copyright © 1999 by Rich and Sue Freeman

Published in the United States of America by Footprint Press

All rights reserved. No part of this book may be reproduced in any form or by any electronic or mechanical means, including storage and retrieval systems, without permission in writing from the publisher:
  Footprint Press, P.O. Box 645, Fishers, NY 14453.

Copy Edited by Irene F. Galvin, Communications Connection
Cover Design by Tamara L. Dever, TLC Graphics
Maps by Rich Freeman
Pictures by Rich & Sue Freeman
Cover Picture provided by Finger Lakes Association (1-800-KIT4FUN)

ISBN 0-9656974-9-5

Manufactured in the United States of America

Library of Congress Catalog Card Number: 99-90038

Every effort has been made to provide accurate and up to date trail descriptions in this book. Hazards are noted where known. Users of this book are reminded that they alone are responsible for their own safety when on any trail and that they use the routes described in this book at their own risk.

The authors, publishers, and distributors of this book assume no responsibility for any injury, misadventure, or loss occurring from use of the information contained herein.

Locations by Trail Number

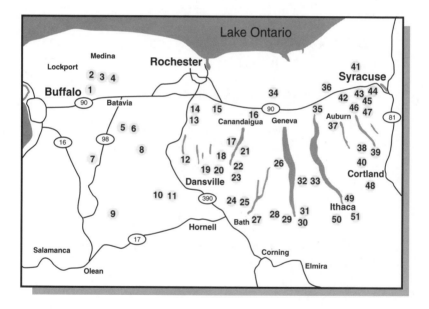

CONTENTS

Walks in Monroe, Ontario, & Yates Counties

Walks in Steuben & Schuyler Counties

Walks in Wayne, Seneca, & Cayuga Counties

Acknowledgments

The research, writing, production, and promotion of a book such as this is never a solitary adventure. *Take A Hike!* came into being because of the assistance of many wonderful people who freely shared their knowledge, experience, resources, thoughts, and time. We extend our heartfelt thanks to them all. Each in his or her own way is responsible for making the Finger Lakes and Genesee Valley Region a better place to live and, most of all, a community rich with the spirit of collaboration for the betterment of all. This is what ensures quality of life within a community. Thank you, each and every one.

Beaver Lake Nature Center (Bruce Stebbins et al)
Beaver Meadow Nature Center (Bill Michalek et al)
Blue Cut Nature Center (Kimberly Gardner et al)
Cayuga County Park and Trails Commission (Michele Beilman
  et al)
Cayuga County Planning Board (Tom Higgins et al)
Cayuga Trails Club
Centers for Nature Education (Elaine Burtless et al)
Central & Western NY Chapter, Nature Conservancy
Cumming Nature Center (Melissa Anderson et al)
Erie County Parks
Fillmore Glen State Park (Thomas Noble et al)
Finger Lakes Association (Laurie Nichiporuk et al)
Finger Lakes Interpretive Center (Mary Beth Livers et al)
Finger Lakes National Forest Ranger District (Martha Twarkins
  et al)
Finger Lakes Trail Conference (Howard Beye, Chuck McLellan,
  Irene Szabo et al)
Finger Lakes Trust (Gay Nicholson et al)
Friends of Genesee Valley Greenway (Fran Gotcsik et al)
Friends of the Outlet (Phil Whitman et al)
Genesee County Park (John Volpe et al)
Iroquois National Wildlife Refuge (Dorothy Gerhart et al)
Lime Hollow Nature Center (Susannah Touchet et al)
Montezuma National Wildlife Refuge (Marva Gingrich et al)

New York State Department of Environmental Conservation
(Jim Carpenter, David Conley, Jim Eckler, Greg Fuerst,
John Hauber, Mark Keister, William Meehan, Jim Peek,
Bruce Penrod, Ron Schroder, Wesley Stiles, Jack Watson, et al)

N.Y.S. Office of Parks, Recreation, & Historic Preservation
(Chris Nielsen et al)

Onanda Park (Sue Dubler et al)

Ontario Pathways (Betsy Russell et al)

Perry Development Committee (E. D. Anna et al)

Sapsucker Woods (Tim Gallagher et al)

Sims' Museum and Camillus Erie Canal Park (David Beebe et al)

Town of Skaneateles (Janet Aaron, Helen Ionta et al)

Victor Hiking Trails (David Wright et al)

Watkins Glen State Park (Robert DeNardo et al)

These people directed us to choice trails, reviewed our maps and descriptions, supplied historical tidbits, and often are responsible for the existence and maintenance of the trails. They have our sincere appreciation.

Introduction

"When the glaciers came they left in their wake a realm of gentle hills. And when the sun rose for the first time upon the new land, a spirit of the earth saw it and thought it so beautiful that he laid his hands upon the ground to bless it. When his hands were moved, the hollows left by his fingers were filled with water."

A local legend provided by the Finger Lakes Interpretive Center

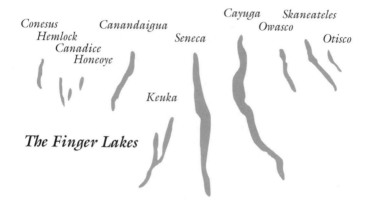

Take a hike or a short walk. It's good for you. In as little as one hour you can do your body a favor – stretch your legs, raise your heart rate, and decrease your stress level. Hiking is a perfect exercise to balance today's hectic lifestyle.

Over the past years we have enjoyed hiking in many states throughout the United States. It didn't matter if it was a brief walk or an extended backpacking trip. Every time we ventured outside, Mother Nature offered something new and wonderful. We learned it's not necessary to go far to reap these benefits.

In 1997 we wrote and published *Take A Hike! Family Walks in the Rochester Area* which described 40 short hikes in Monroe and Ontario Counties. We were heartened by the reaction to that book. Families used it

11

to expose their kids to the abundance of nature, people of all ages and abilities used it as part of an exercise program, and newcomers used it to learn about the area. As we continued hiking, we'd pass people on trails with our book clasped tightly in their hands. Generally the book looked tattered and well-worn. It always made us smile. People were using the resource we so lovingly provided.

So, here is the next book in the series. For people of the Rochester area it can be a way to continue exploring once you've finished all the trails in the first book. For people in the wider Finger Lakes and Genesee Valley Region, we hope the short trails in this book lead you to new horizons. If you want even longer trails, please check out *Take Your Bike! Family Rides in the Finger Lakes & Genesee Valley Region*. It's chock full of long trails which are great for hiking as well as bicycling.

Many of the trails in this book were built and are maintained by volunteer or community groups. They all welcome new members. We encourage everyone to join and benefit from the wide range of resources available in the Finger Lakes and Genesee Valley Region.

Most trails listed in this book are free and open to the public. A few require a small admission fee or request a donation. They are clearly noted in the heading to each trail beside the term "Admission." You do not have to be a member of the sponsoring group to enjoy any of the trails.

If you find inaccurate information or substantially different conditions (after all, things do change), please send a note detailing your findings to:

Footprint Press, P.O. Box 645, Fishers, NY 1445
or e-mail us through our web site: http://www.footprintpress.com

How To Use This Book

We have clustered the hikes into seven groups using county boundaries as groupings and working west to east:

> Walks in Erie & Genesee Counties
> Walks in Wyoming, Allegany, & Livingston Counties
> Walks in Monroe, Ontario, & Yates Counties
> Walks in Steuben & Schuyler Counties
> Walks in Wayne, Seneca, & Cayuga Counties
> Walks in Onondaga County
> Walks in Tompkins & Cortland Counties

We selected the trails with variety in mind. Some of the better known trails are popular and heavily traveled, but their splendor (like Watkins Glen) made it hard for us to leave them out. Most of the trails are lesser known and lightly traveled. We also selected trails which are fairly easy to follow or well marked. Areas with many intersecting trails (where we got lost) were excluded.

Where possible, we have designated hikes that go in a loop to let you see as much as possible without backtracking. You can easily begin and end in one location and not worry about finding transportation back to the beginning.

Approximate hiking times are given, but of course this depends on your speed. If you stop to watch the wildlife, enjoy the views, or read the descriptive plaques, it will take you longer than the time given. You'll notice that many of the hikes also have shortcuts or are connected to other trails that allow you to adjust your time.

The maps for each trail are just sketches. We wanted maps that were easy to view and understand so everyone could be comfortable looking at where they were going and what they were seeing. Some of the sketches were taken from more detailed maps showing overall general location relative to intersecting trails and landscape features. Some areas were never mapped for hiking trails prior to this book.

Legend

At the beginning of each trail listing, you will find a map and description with the following information:

Location: The closest town or lake and the county the trail is in.

Directions: How to find the trailhead parking area from a major road or town.

Alternative Parking: Other parking locations with access to the trail. Use these if you want to shorten your hike by starting or stopping at a spot other than the designated endpoint.

Hiking Time: Approximate time to hike at a comfortable pace, including time to enjoy the views.

Length: The round-trip length of the hike in miles (unless noted as one-way).

Difficulty:

(1 boot) easy hiking, generally level trail

(2 boots) rolling hills, gradual grades on trail

(3 boots) gentle climbing required to follow the trail

(4 boots) some strenuous climbing required

Surface: The materials that make up the trail surface for the major portion of the hike.

Trail Markings: Markings used to designate the trails in this book vary widely. Some trails are not marked at all but can be followed by cleared or worn paths. This doesn't pose a problem for the hiker as long as there aren't many intersecting, unmarked paths. Other trails are well marked with either signs, blazes, or markers, and

14

sometimes a combination of all three. Blazing is done by the official group that maintains the trail.

Signs – wooden or metal signs with instructions in words or pictures.

Blazes – painted markings on trees showing where the trail goes. Many blazes are rectangular and placed at eye level. (See the picture on page 126.) Colors may be used to denote different trails. If a tree has twin blazes beside one another, you should proceed cautiously because the trail either turns or another trail intersects.

Sometimes you'll see a section of trees with painted markings which aren't neat geometric shapes. These are probably boundary markers or trees marked for logging. Trail blazes are generally distinct geometric shapes and are placed at eye level.

Markers – small plastic or metal geometric shapes (square, round, triangular) nailed to trees at eye level to show where the trail goes. They also may be colored to denote different trails.

It is likely that at some point you will lose the blazes or markers while following a trail. The first thing to do is stop and look around. See if you can spot a blaze or marker by looking in all directions, including behind you. If not, backtrack until you see a blaze or marker, then proceed forward again, carefully following the markings.

Uses: Each trail has a series of icons depicting the activity or activities allowed on the trail. Jogging is allowed on all trails, as is snowshoeing when snow covers the ground.

The icons include:

Hiking	Bicycling	Cross-country Skiing
Wheelchairs	Horseback Riding	Snow-mobiling

Contact: The address and phone number of the orgnization to contact if you would like additional information or if you have questions not answered in this book.

Map Legend

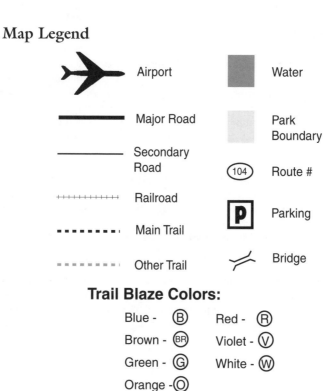

✈	Airport	▪	Water
▬	Major Road	▪	Park Boundary
───	Secondary Road	(104)	Route #
++++++++++	Railroad	**P**	Parking
▪ ▪ ▪ ▪ ▪ ▪	Main Trail	⤢	Bridge
▪ ▪ ▪ ▪ ▪	Other Trail		

Trail Blaze Colors:

Blue - Ⓑ   Red - Ⓡ

Brown - ⓑⓡ   Violet - Ⓥ

Green - Ⓖ   White - Ⓦ

Orange - Ⓞ

Directions

In the directions we often tell you to turn left or right. To avoid confusion, in some instances we have noted a compass direction in parentheses according to the following:

(N) = north
(S) = south
(E) = east
(W) = west

Some trails have "Y" or "T" junctions. A "Y" junction indicates one path that turns into two paths. The direction we give is either bear left or bear right. A "T" junction is one path that ends at another. The direction is turn left or turn right.

Guidelines

Any adventure in the outdoors can be inherently dangerous. It's important to watch where you are going and keep an eye on children. Some of these trails are on private property where permission is benevolently granted by the landowners. Please respect the landowners and their property. Follow all regulations posted on signs and stay on the trails. Our behavior today will determine how many of these wonderful trails remain for future generations to enjoy.

Follow "no-trace" ethics whenever you venture outdoors. "No-trace" ethics means that the only thing left behind as evidence of your passing is your footprints. Carry out all trash you carry in. Do not litter. In fact, carry a plastic bag with you and pick up any litter you happen upon along the way. The trails included in this book are intended for day hikes. Please, no camping or fires.

As the trails age and paths become worn, trail work groups sometimes reroute the trails. This helps control erosion and allows vegetation to return. It also means that if a sign or marker doesn't appear as it is described in the book, it's probably due to trail improvement.

Remember:

Take only pictures, leave only footprints.

Please do not pick anything.

Preparations and Safety

You can enhance your time in the outdoors by dressing properly and carrying appropriate equipment. Even for a short day hike, take a small backpack or fanny pack with the following gear:

camera	flashlight
binoculars	insect spray or lotion
compass	water bottle with water
rain gear	nature guidebook(s) of flowers, birds, etc.
snacks	plastic bag to pick up trash

Many of the trails can be muddy. It's best to wear lightweight hiking boots or at least sturdy sneakers.

Walking sticks have been around for centuries, but they are finding new life and new forms in recent years. These sticks can be anything from a branch picked up along the trail to a $200 pair of poles designed with built-in springs and hand-molded grips. Using a walking stick is a good idea, especially in hilly terrain. It can take the pressure off your knees and help you balance when crossing bridges or logs.

Hiking with children is good exercise as well as an opportunity for learning. Use the time to teach children how to read a compass, identify flowers, trees, birds, and animal tracks. You'll find books on each of these subjects in the public library.

Make it fun by taking a different type of gorp for each hike. Gorp is any combination of dried foods that you eat as a snack. Examples are:

1) peanuts, M&M's®, and raisins
2) chocolate morsels, nuts, and granola
3) dried banana chips, sunflower seeds, and carob chips

Get creative and mix any combination of chocolate, carob, dried fruits, nuts, oats, granolas, etc. The bulk food section at your local grocery store is a wealth of ideas. Other fun snacks are marshmallows, popcorn, peanuts in shells, graham crackers, and beef jerky.

When hiking with a child, tie a string on a whistle and have your child wear it as a necklace for safety. Instruct your child to blow the whistle only if he or she is lost.

19

Dogs Welcome!

Hiking with dogs can be fun because of their keen sense of smell and different perspective on the world. Many times they find things that we would have passed by. They're inquisitive about everything and make excellent companions. But to ensure that your hiking companion enjoys the time outside, you must control your dog. Dogs are required to be leashed on most maintained public trails. The reasons are numerous, but the top ones are to protect dogs, to protect other hikers, and to ensure your pet doesn't chase wildlife. Good dog manners go a long way toward creating goodwill and improving tolerance toward their presence.

Forty-two of the trails listed in this book welcome dogs. Please respect the requirement that dogs be leashed where noted. The only trails which prohibit dogs are:

Trail #	Trail Name
7	Beaver Meadow Nature Center
9	Moss Lake
17	Onanda Park
18	Cumming Nature Center
29	Watkins Glen State Park
41	Beaver Lake Nature Center
44	Camillus Forest Unique Area
47	Baltimore Woods
49	Sapsucker Woods

Seasons

Most people head into the great outdoors in summer. Temperatures are warm, the days are long, and plants and wildlife are plentiful. Summer is a great time to go hiking. But don't neglect the other seasons. Each season offers a unique perspective, and makes hiking the same trail a totally different adventure. In spring, a time of rebirth, you can watch the leaves unfurl and the spring flowers burst.

Become a leaf peeper in fall. Venture forth onto the trails and take in the colorful splendor of a beautiful fall day. Listen to the rustle of newly fallen leaves under your feet and inhale the unique smell of this glorious season.

The only complication with fall is that it coincides with the hunting season. Many of the trails in this guide book are on public lands where hunting is permitted. When hiking in the fall, be sure to wear bright colors and if possible select hiking locations which are not on hunting grounds. The hunting season around the Finger Lakes and Genesee Valley Region is generally:

Archery hunting: mid-October to mid-December
Shotgun hunting: mid-November to mid-December

And, finally, winter. It may be cold out, but the leaves are off the trees and the views will never be better. You can more fully appreciate the variety of this area's terrain if you wander out in winter. It is also the perfect time to watch for animal tracks in the snow and test your identification skills.

21

Land Types

The walks detailed in this book traverse a variety of public and private lands. Regardless of ownership, the land deserves our respect and care. Please tread lightly, stay on the trails, obey posted regulations, and carry out everything carried in.

The New York State Department of Conservation (D.E.C.) and the National Forest Service employ foresters and biologists to oversee lands managed for various purposes. A century ago, only 26% of New York State was covered by forest. Today, 62% is forested.

National and State Forests: Since 1929, when New York State began purchasing and reforesting abandoned farmland, foresters have changed this once-depleted land into the finest forests in the state. The 700,000 acres of state forests and multiple use areas give New Yorkers improved water quality, a sustainable wood supply, and the opportunity for a wide variety of outdoor recreational experiences. Foresters also manage these lands to provide a diversity of wildlife habitats and to protect and enhance populations of rare and endangered species.

Unique Areas: D.E.C. purchases unique areas to preserve unusual ecosystems. An example is the Camillus Unique Area where a nearly old growth forest is being saved for posterity.

Wildlife Management Areas and Wildlife Refuges: These areas are dedicated to perpetuating wildlife species, demonstrating management practices, and providing wildlife-related recreational activities. Wildlife biologists and foresters work together to manage the 175,000 acres which make up the State's Wildlife Management Areas.

Many other lands are opened to hikers through the hard work and generous spirit of government agencies, conservation and nature societies, and a myriad of volunteers.

State, County, Town, and City Parks: These lands are generally developed for public recreational uses. They often have nature or intrepretive centers, shelters or pavilions, restrooms, picnic facilities, and other amenities.

Nature Preserves and Nature Centers: These privately owned lands are often open for public use. They are managed by organizations such as nature conservancies, land trusts, Aububon Societies, and museums.

Organizations: The Finger Lakes and Genesee Valley Region is blessed to have volunteer organizations that either purchase lands to develop trail systems or work with private landowners to obtain permission for trails to cross private lands. These include organizations such as Ontario Pathways, Victor Hiking Trails, Cayuga Trails Club, Friends of the Finger Lakes Outlet, Friends of Blue Cut, and Finger Lakes Trail Conference.

Finger Lakes Trail
and Connecting Trails

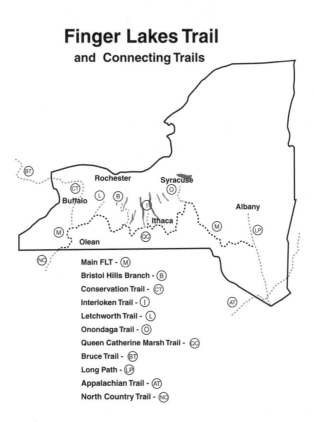

Main FLT - (M)
Bristol Hills Branch - (B)
Conservation Trail - (CT)
Interloken Trail - (I)
Letchworth Trail - (L)
Onondaga Trail - (O)
Queen Catherine Marsh Trail - (QC)
Bruce Trail - (BT)
Long Path - (LP)
Appalachian Trail - (AT)
North Country Trail - (NC)

The Finger Lakes Trail Conference is unique in the scope of its endeavors within the area. The Finger Lakes Trail stretches for 559 miles from Allegheny State Park in southwestern New York State, across the bottom of the Finger Lakes, into the Catskill Mountains north of New York City. Part of it is also the North Country National Scenic Trail which will eventually span from North Dakota to eastern New York State. The Finger Lakes Trail connects with the Long Path which connects with the Appalachian Trail. At the western end, by way of the Conservation Trail it connects to the Bruce Trail. The Finger Lakes Trail has six branch trails totalling 238 miles, creating an extensive trail network.

Eight trails in this guide include segments of the Finger Lakes Trail. They are:

Trail	Trail Name	Length
#23	Hi Tor Wildlife Management Area	4.5 miles
#25	Urbana State Forest – Long Loop	7.1 miles
#27	Birdseye Hollow State Forest	2.0 miles
#28	Goundry Hill State Forest	4.5 miles
#29	Watkins Glen State Park	3.0 miles
#31	Texas Hollow State Forest	4.1 miles
#33	Finger Lakes National Forest – Gorge Trail	5.4 miles
#50	Sweedler Preserve	1.6 miles

Hike the 32.2 miles of these eight trails and you are eligible for a 3.5-inch FLT – Footprint Press Patch:

To order your patch, send your name, address, and a check for $4.00 to:

Finger Lakes Trail Conference
FLT – Footprint Press Patch
P.O. Box 18048
Rochester, NY 14618-0048

or phone your order to (716) 288-7191
and charge it to your VISA or MasterCard

All 800 plus miles of the Finger Lakes Trail System and its campsites are open to the public for hiking adventures. It is built and maintained entirely by volunteers with financial support from membership dues and map and guidebook sales. Ask at the above F.L.T.C. address for a map buyer's guide or membership information.

Walks in Erie & Genesee Counties

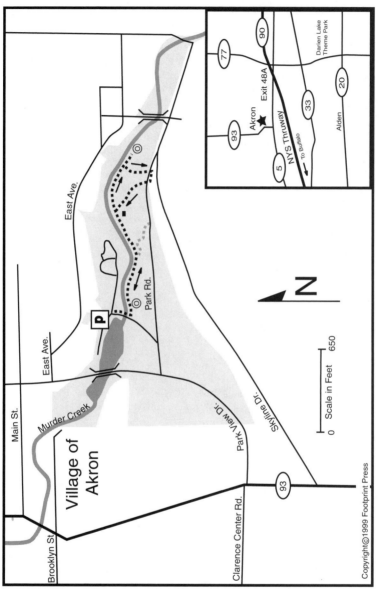

Akron Falls Park

1.
Akron Falls Park

Location:	Akron, (west of Batavia), Erie County
Directions:	From Route 5, head north on Route 93. Pass Skyline Drive and turn right on Park View Drive. Turn right at the sign for Akron Falls Park. Turn left at the stop sign and head downhill, over a bridge. Parking is to the left, past the bridge.

Alternative Parking: None

Hiking Time:	30 minutes
Length:	0.5 mile loop
Difficulty:	🐾 🐾 🐾 🐾 🐾 🐾
Surface:	Dirt trail and paved path
Trail Markings:	Wooden sign at trailhead, some orange blazes
Uses:	🚶
Dogs:	OK on leash
Admission:	Free
Contact:	Akron Falls Park (716) 542-2330
	Erie County Parks 95 Franklin Street Buffalo, NY 14202 (716) 858-8352

This park is a picnickers haven. It's loaded with tables, grills, swings, jungle gyms, the gurgle of a flowing creek, and the shade of large trees. Who'd suspect that this docile waterway is called Murder Creek? Akron Falls Park is a 284-acre county park. The trail climbs through the woods to a waterfall where the waters of Murder Creek slip though the rocks and plummet over the Onondaga Escarpment.

Western New York has three major escarpments or rock ledges. They are roughly parallel, north-facing ledges. The best known is the Niagara Escarpment, which forms Niagara Falls. Sixteen miles south, the Onondaga

Akron Falls

Escarpment ranges from 30 to 70 feet high as it crosses western New York from Buffalo. The southern-most escarpment is the Portage or Lake Erie Escarpment, which forms the northern border of the Allegheny Plateau.

You'll notice orange blazes along this trail. You're walking a segment of the Conservation Trail, which connects the Finger Lakes Trail in Allegany State Park to the Bruce Trail near Niagara Falls, Canada. The park is open from 7:00 AM until 9:00 PM daily.

Campgrounds: Darien Lakes Theme Park & Camping Resort, 9993 Allegheny Road, Darien Center, (716) 599-2211

Darien Lakes State Park, 10289 Harlow Road, Darien Center, (800) 456-2267

Ice Cream: The Craving Shop, Main Street, downtown Akron

Trail Directions
- Walk across the bridge from the parking area.
- Turn left under a wooden "Nature Trail" sign.
- Continue straight past a trail to the right. The creek is on your left.
- Pass pavilion #9.
- Pass an old asphalt road to the right. (This will be your return loop.)
- After 0.2 mile, the trail becomes rough paved and heads uphill.
- An old stone wall will line the trail.
- Pass a trail to the right.
- Shortly the trail ends at an observation area. Akron Falls cascades from among the rocks in front of you.
- Return along the stone wall, but bear left at the first junction and head uphill.
- Walk to Park Road, cross the road and turn right.

29

- At 0.3 mile, you'll find the rock garden on your left. Stroll through the walkways of the garden.
- Walk back across Park Road and head downhill on the old road, which is now blocked from traffic.
- Bear left at the bottom of the hill and pass pavilion #9.
- Pass a trail to the left.
- At 0.5 mile, reach the road. Turn right to cross the bridge to the parking area.

Date Hiked: _____

Notes:

Iroquois National Wildlife Refuge

At the end of the last glacial period, a huge lake called Tonawanda covered what is now Iroquois National Wildlife Refuge. With the passage of time, the lake receded and plants encroached to form marshes. Marshes filled to become moist meadows and meadows became woods and swamp. Centuries later, the Seneca Indians cleared much of the oak forest for farming. The first European settlers likened the remaining clusters of oak trees to orchards and so named the area "Oak Orchard Swamp."

The ancient swamps were artificially drained through the 1800s and early 1900s to enhance logging and farming operations. Due to the high cost of drainage, recurring muck fires, and floods, these programs proved to be marginal at best. By the 1930s, residents noticed a sharp decline in the once plentiful wildlife and made plans to protect the dwindling swamp from further development.

Western New York lies along the Atlantic Flyway, a major north/south route traveled by migrating birds. This area, with its combination of marshes, open waters, and croplands, has historically been a major staging, resting, nesting, and feeding area for ducks, geese, and other migratory birds. In 1958 the federal government established the Oak Orchard National Wildlife Refuge. To avoid confusion with the neighboring Oak Orchard State Wildlife Management Area, the refuge was renamed Iroquois National Wildlife Refuge in 1964, in honor of the Iroquois Nation. Many areas of the refuge are namesakes of these early inhabitants.

Today the Iroquois National Wildlife Refuge encompasses 10,818 acres of wooded swamps, marshlands, wet meadows, pasture, and cropland. It is bordered to the east by Oak Orchard State Wildlife Management Area and to the west by Tonawanda State Wildlife Management Area. Wetland habitats were restored through the construction of perimeter dikes to create large impoundments of marsh vegetation. To provide the best possible habitat for wildlife, water levels in the impoundments are manipulated to create conditions that provide a mix of underwater plants, emergent vegetation, and open water.

Natural, undisturbed marshes thrive because of fluctuating water levels. The fluctuations usually result from precipitation or lack of it. Periodic drying is important for the longevity of a marsh. During dry times the marsh soil is exposed to air which allows it to consolidate, thus providing a good foothold for new plants. Dead organic matter decomposes and replenishes nutrients for growing plants. The dried soil provides an excellent bed for seed germination.

Iroquois National Wildlife Refuge is one of over 500 refuges in the U.S. managed specifically for the protection of wildlife and wildlife habitat. It is administered by the U.S. Fish and Wildlife Service. A nature center is open weekdays from 7:30 AM until 4:00 PM at the headquarters on Casey Road. It has bird and animal displays, a bird nest observation scope, and restrooms.

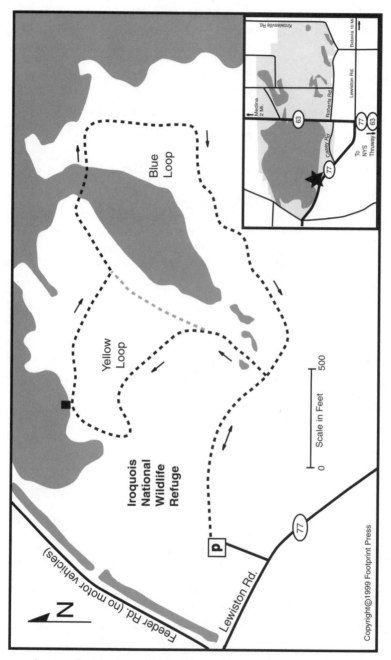

Iroquois National Wildlife Refuge - Kanyoo Trail

2.
Iroquois National Wildlife Refuge
Kanyoo Trail

Location: Iroquois National Wildlife Refuge, Alabama, (north
                       west of Batavia), Genesee County
Directions: The parking area is on the north side of Route 77
                       (Lewiston Road) between Casey Road and Salt Works
                       Road. It's marked with a large brown and white sign
                       for "Kanyoo Trail" and has brown and white mainte-
                       nance buildings at the back of the parking lot.
Alternative Parking: None
Hiking Time: 30 minutes
Length: 1.1 mile loop
Difficulty:

Surface: Gravel and packed dirt trails
Trail Markings: Blue and yellow markers
Uses:

Dogs: OK on leash
Admission: Free
Contact: Iroquois National Wildlife Refuge
                       1101 Casey Road
                       Bascom, NY 14013
                       (716) 948-5445

This is an easy-to-follow, shaded woods walk. It takes you back to a marsh
observation platform and along a raised boardwalk over cattails. Numbered
guideposts along the way help you understand your natural surroundings.
Here is the explanation for the guideposts as provided by the Department
of the Interior, U.S. Fish and Wildlife Service:

1. Habitat Management: This refuge is managed to meet the habitat
needs of many different animals. Mowing and fire keep brush from taking
over grassy fields. Mallards, pheasants, and blue-winged teal nest here while
deer and other animals hide or rest in the grass. Eastern bluebirds typically

34

nest in knotholes in wooden fence posts or in dead trees. Nesting boxes, such as this one, replace natural nest sites lost to development.

2. A Helping Hand: For centuries farmers have planted hedgerows to mark the boundaries between fields or properties. Then, as now, birds and small mammals find food and shelter in the shrubs and trees of a hedgerow. Hedgerows also form a transition zone between two different habitats, such as fields and woods.

3. Living Together: Vines use trees as ladders to reach the sunlight. In commensalism, one species (the vine) benefits without harming the other (the tree). Vines make good hiding places or nesting spots for birds. What are they?

> Poison Ivy – look for three leaflets growing from a common stem. No leaves? Look for hairy-looking stems climbing up a tree trunk. The "hair" is aerial roots. In open areas poison ivy can look like a shrub. Birds eat the clusters of white berries in the fall. WARNING: all parts of this plant are poisonous to people and can cause a severe rash if touched.

> Virginia Creeper – has five leaflets arranged like the spokes of a wheel on a smooth stem. Small, greenish flowers in the summer produce blue-black berries in the fall and winter.

> Wild Grape – woody stems and heart-shaped leaves are characteristic of wild grapevines. Birds and other small animals eat the clusters of small purple grapes.

4. Black Cherry: Identified by its "cornflake" bark, the black cherry is a valuable hardwood tree in these woods. Songbirds, deer, rabbits, and mice all eat the clusters of small dark cherries. The seeds (pits), which are not digestible, passed through the digestive system of animals, germinated, and grew where they landed, creating this grove.

5. Vernal Pool: "Vernal" means spring. This seasonal wetland is a nursery for frogs and other amphibians. This is also a recycling center. When the flooded trees become diseased they are attacked by insects, which in turn are eaten by woodpeckers and other birds. Mushrooms, mosses, and small animals such as millipedes, worms, and sowbugs break the dead wood down into minerals, which will nourish the next generation of plants.

6. In The "Thicket" Of It: Communities undergo a cycle called succession in which one group of plants and animals replaces another. Shrubs

35

shade out the shorter plants (herbs or grasses) which in turn are shaded out by taller plants (trees) which are overshadowed by even taller trees. Each species changes the habitat so that other plant and animal species can move in and take over. Finally, in a climax community, a few species dominate the community and replace themselves.

7. Tulip Trees: Both the leaves and the flowers resemble a tulip. Also known as yellow poplar, the tulip tree is more closely related to the magnolia. Let your eyes follow the gray-brown ridges and furrows up the straight, limbless trunk to the top. This is one of the largest of our eastern hardwoods. Still valued for its cheap and easily worked lumber, it was once used by Native Americans to make dugout canoes. Around the base of the tree, look for evidence that squirrels and chipmunks have been feasting on the compact, cone-like clusters of seeds.

8. Adaptation: In wetlands, where the water table is high, some trees will send their roots out sideways just below the surface. Without strong anchors, the force of the wind felled these trees.

9. In The Eye of the Beholder: What do wild turkeys, fruit baskets, and vandals have in common? Answer: beech trees. Turkeys search the ground for the small, triangular nuts; fruit baskets were once made from strips of the wood; and vandals deface the smooth, gray bark. Not only does cutting into the bark make these trees vulnerable to disease, it is vandalism, and is against the law. Unlike other deciduous trees, beech trees will hold onto their brown leaves until spring, making them easy trees to spot in the winter woods.

10. The Value Of Wetlands: For a long time wetlands have been considered worthless havens for mosquitoes, but wetlands control floods by acting like a sponge, soaking up large amounts of water from storms or spring thaws. Wetland plants reduce erosion by slowing the rate of water flow. Wetlands help filter pollutants from water and recharge groundwater supplies. In Iroquois Refuge, marshes such as this are actively managed for resting, feeding, staging, and nesting areas for migratory waterfowl and other water birds. Wetlands are a unique ecosystem. Stop, look, and listen to the beauty of a wetland.

Trail Directions
• Head east on the gravel path from the parking area.
• Turn left at guidepost #4.
• At 0.1 mile, turn left onto the yellow blazed trail.

36

- At 0.3 mile, reach an observation platform overlooking the marsh. Guidepost #10 is on the left.
- The gravel ends and the trail becomes packed dirt.
- At 0.4 mile, bear left on the blue trail. (The yellow trail heads right.)
- Cross the raised boardwalk, giving you a view over the tops of the cattail marsh.
- At 1.0 mile, turn left (W) to return to the parking lot.

Date Hiked: _____

Notes:

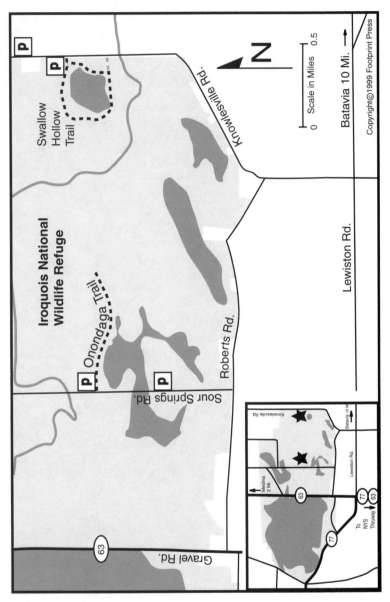

Iroquois National Wildlife Refuge
Onondaga Trail & Swallow Hollow Trail

3.
Iroquois National Wildlife Refuge
Onondaga Trail

Location:	Iroquois National Wildlife Refuge, Alabama, (north west of Batavia), Genesee County
Directions:	From Batavia, follow Route 63 north. Turn east on Roberts Road and north on Sour Springs Road. The parking area, on the east side of Sour Springs Road, is marked with a large brown and white sign for "Onondaga Nature Trail." A white house is across the street.

Alternative Parking: None

Hiking Time:	1.25 hours
Length:	2.4 mile round trip
Difficulty:	👣 👣
Surface:	Gravel and packed dirt trails
Trail Markings:	None
Uses:	🚶 🥢
Dogs:	OK on leash
Admission:	Free
Contact:	Iroquois National Wildlife Refuge
	1101 Casey Road
	Bascom, NY 14013
	(716) 948-5445

After a short walk on the dike of Onondaga Pool, this trail enters a mixed woods of maple, aspen, and pine. Because of hunting in the area, this trail is closed to hiking during shotgun deer hunting season.

Trail Directions
- From the parking area, head southeast on the grass path past a brown metal gate.
- The trail soon turns to white gravel as you cross the dike by Onondaga

Walking the dike along Onondaga Pool

Pool. Pause to watch the turtles lounging on logs and ducks slowly paddling by.
- At 0.4 mile, enter the woods. The trail turns to packed dirt.
- Pass a bench along the trail.
- At 1.0 mile, pass a second bench.
- The trail ends after 1.2 mile, at a third bench. Turn around and retrace your path back to the parking area.

Date Hiked: _____

Notes:

4.
Iroquois National Wildlife Refuge
Swallow Hollow Trail

Location: Iroquois National Wildlife Refuge, Alabama, (north
                     west of Batavia), Genesee County
Directions: From Batavia, follow Route 63 north. Turn east on
                     Roberts Road and north on Knowlesville Road. The
                     parking area is on the west side of Knowlesville Road.
Alternative Parking: None
Hiking Time: 45 minutes
Length: 1.4 mile loop
Difficulty: 👣 👣

Surface: Packed dirt trails and raised boardwalks
Trail Markings: None, but an easy-to-follow trail
Uses: 🥾

Dogs: OK on leash
Admission: Free
Contact: Iroquois National Wildlife Refuge
                     1101 Casey Road
                     Bascom, NY 14013
                     (716) 948-5445

On this unique trail, you'll be raised five feet off the floor of Swallow
Hollow Marsh for 0.4 mile on a boardwalk. It can be slippery when wet,
but affords an unusual vantage point for the wetlands below. See the map
on page 38.

Trail Directions
- From the southwest corner of the parking area, head south onto a
  boardwalk raised five feet above the Swallow Hollow Marsh.
- After 0.1 mile, reach a pond to the right and continue through the
  marsh high on the boardwalk.
- Reach a "T" at 0.2 mile and turn right on a gravel dike. (0.2 mile to the

left is Knowlesville Road.)
- At 0.5 mile, the trail bends right (NE). It winds into the woods and gradually heads uphill.
- Cross two small wooden bridges, then enter a pine forest.
- Cross a third small wooden bridge, then return to a deciduous forest.
- At 0.9 mile, cross a long wooden bridge.
- Reach the raised boardwalk at 1.1 mile. It will lead you back to the parking area.

The boardwalk of
Swallow Hollow Trail

Date Hiked: _____
Notes:

Genesee County Park and Forest

Genesee County Park and Forest is the first and oldest county forest in New York State and owes its existence to the poor and lunatic people of Genesee County. In 1927 and 1928, Genesee County opened a home for the poor and a residence for the care and confinement of lunatics. Some of the old buildings can still be seen on the corner of Bethany Center Road and Raymond Road.

The poor included orphans, habitual drunkards, and paupers, which included any person who was blind, lame, old, decrepit, or vagrant. Lunatics were described as persons who had understanding but by disease, grief, or other accident, lost the use of reason. It also included anyone of unsound mind due to old age, sickness, or weakness who was unable to manage their own affairs.

In 1882 the county purchased a wood lot to supply the cooking and heating needs of the "Poor House Farm" and sold wood for $0.75 a cord to cover expenses. In 1915, 31,000 trees were planted at a cost of $225, beginning the establishment of the forest. These were supplemented with evergreens in the 1920s. By 1935, 169,000 trees had been planted and the land was designated the first county forest in New York State.

Through the 1940s, 1950s, and 1960s, the county supervisors studied and discussed plans for a park. It wasn't until 1966 that funds were finally allocated. The Genesee County Park and Forest became a reality in 1971.

Today it is a gem rivaled by few others. Expanses of forest are interspersed with picnic areas, toboggan hills, horseshoe pits, volleyball courts, sandboxes, playgrounds, and baseball fields. Over the years many volunteer groups have contributed to the development of this park. In 1998, a group from Job Corps joined local volunteers to build a stunning nature center complete with stuffed animals and natural exhibits. Volunteers offer a variety of nature programs on subjects ranging from turtles to blue birds to

43

backyard composting. The nature center is open from 3:30 PM to 9:00 PM weekdays and 9:00 AM to 9:00 PM on weekends.

The park is open daily from 9:00 AM until 9:00 PM. It includes a unique Braille and large-print nature trail near Raymond Road in Area A. This walking-only trail is bordered by a coated link railing so the blind can walk along the trail and read the Braille interpretive signs. Unfortunately, as is true throughout the park, some of the signs have been disturbed by vandalism. The county continually works on replacing signage in the park.

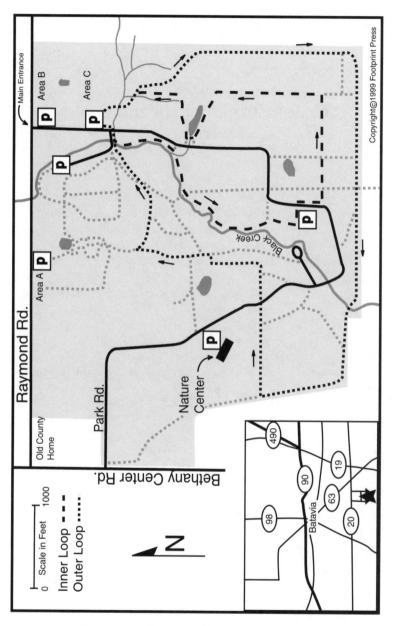

Genesee County Park and Forest

5.
Genesee County Park and Forest Outer Loop

Location: Bethany, (south of Batavia, bordering the Wyoming
                   County boundary), Genesee County

Directions: From Route 20, turn south on Bethany Center Road.
                   Turn east on Raymond Road. Turn south off Raymond
                   Road through the main park entrance onto Park Road.
                   Park at the second parking area on the left (Area C).

Alternative Parking: The first parking area (Area B)

Hiking Time: 1.5 hour

Length: 2.9 mile loop (combine with the inner loop trail for a
                   4.7 mile loop)

Difficulty: 👣 👣 👣 👣

Surface: Dirt and grass trails

Trail Markings: Some junction number signs and some trail name signs

Uses: 🚶 🚴 🎿 🐎 🛷

Dogs: OK on leash

Admission: Free

Contact: Genesee County Park and Forest
                   11095 Bethany Center Road
                   East Bethany, NY 14054
                   (716) 344-1122

The outer loop trail is partially in the woods and partially through wide,
mowed swaths which can be warm when the sun is strong. It's challenging
because of the hilly terrain and the mowed grass trails. This trail takes you
into a less heavily used area of the park.

Bed and Breakfast: Roaring Creek Lodge B&B, 2761 West Main Street
                   Road, Batavia, (716) 762-8881

Campgrounds: Lei-Ti Campground, 9979 Francis Road, Batavia,
                   (800) 445-3484

                   Golden Mobile Campground, 5610 East Main Street
                   Road, Batavia, (800) 528-9651

Trail Directions (designated by the short, dark, dashed lines on the map)

- From the second parking area (Area C), head south past a pavilion on the dirt trail.
- Bear left at the first junction and head uphill.
- Cross two small wooden bridges and continue uphill after each.
- Pass a small trail off to the right.
- At 0.8 mile, the trail turns right on a wide grass path. The trail will be a gradual downhill.
- Continue straight past two trails to the right.
- Continue straight through a trail intersection.
- At 1.2 miles, another trail will head off to the right. Continue straight, uphill.
- Cross two culverts, then pass a trail to the right.
- Climb a steep hill. At the top of the hill the trail bends right, then heads down. The trees to your right are Norway spruce.
- At 1.8 miles, turn right and head downhill on another grass trail. To your left is a forest of white cedar.
- Cross a small wooden bridge. The county plans to build a pond in the lowland to your right.
- Pass a trail to the right and continue uphill.
- At 2 miles, cross Park Road. Continue uphill on the grass path.
- Pass a woods trail on the right.
- At 2.2 miles, reach trail junction #6 (Wilderness Trail). Bear left on the Forestry Trail.
- Pass the second branch of the Wilderness Trail to the right. Stay on the Forestry Trail (green blazed).
- Soon, reach another junction, and stay right on the Forestry Trail.
- The trail narrows, turns into dirt, and heads downhill through the woods.
- Turn right on the Conservation Trail (blue blazed) before a small wooden bridge.
- Enter a pine forest. Continue straight past a trail to the right.
- At 2.6 miles, continue straight (S) through junction #16.
- At 2.8 miles, turn right (SE) on a road. Cross a bridge over Black Creek. [To combine with the inner loop trail, turn right on the dirt trail after the bridge.]
- Turn left at the stop sign onto Park Road.
- The parking area is a quick right.

Date Hiked: _____

Notes:

6.

Genesee County Park and Forest
Inner Loop

Location: Bethany, (south of Batavia bordering the Wyoming
                     County boundary), Genesee County
Directions: Turn south off Raymond Road through the main park
                     entrance onto Park Road. Park at the second parking
                     area on the left (Area C).
Alternative Parking: The first parking area (Area B)
Hiking Time: 2 hours
Length: 1.8 mile loop (combine with the outer loop trail for a
                     4.7 mile loop)
Difficulty: 🦶 🦶 🦶 🦶

Surface: Dirt and gravel trails with roots
Trail Markings: Some junction number signs and some trail name signs
Uses: 🚶 🚴 🎿 🐎 🛷

Dogs: OK on leash
Admission: Free
Contact: Genesee County Park and Forest
                     11095 Bethany Center Road
                     East Bethany, NY 14054
                     (716) 344-1122

This inner loop trail takes you through hilly terrain in the woods. Sometimes it's on narrow trails along Black Creek and sometimes on wide trails, but always shaded by a canopy of trees. Choose this route for a hot or sunny day. Besides the hills, the challenge comes from walking over roots across the trail. Refer to the map on page 45.

Bed and Breakfast: Roaring Creek Lodge B&B, 2761 West Main Street
                   Road, Batavia, (716) 762-8881

Campgrounds: Lei-Ti Campground, 9979 Francis Road, Batavia,
                    (800) 445-3484

                    Golden Mobile Campground, 5610 East Main
                    Street, Batavia, (800) 528-9651

Trail Directions (designated by the long, dark dashed lines
                    on the map on page 45)

• From the second parking area (Area C), head left (S) on Park Road.
• Turn a quick right on the paved road.
• Immediately before the bridge, turn left onto the trail.
• Cross a cement bridge. This narrow gravel trail through the woods
  follows Black Creek.
• At the trail junction, bear right and cross a boardwalk.
• Continue straight (SW) through a trail intersection. The terrain now gets
  hilly.
• Bear right at a "Y" junction and head uphill.
• At 0.7 mile, reach a parking area and turn left.
• Turn right onto Park Road.
• In 0.1 mile, take the first left (E), on a wide dirt trail, shaded by the
  woods.
• Continue straight through two intersections.
• At 1.1 mile, you'll reach a "T". Turn left (N).
• The terrain continues to be hilly. Pass a swamp to the right.
• Turn right in front of the pavilion. (If you reach the road, you walked
  too far.)
• Now a steep uphill to a "T." Turn right and continue uphill.
• The terrain will be hilly.
• Reach another "T." Turn left (NW).
    [To combine this with the outer loop, turn right at the "T."]
• Pass a pavilion and cross a creek to the parking area.

Date Hiked: _____

Notes:

Walks in Wyoming, Allegany, & Livingston Counties

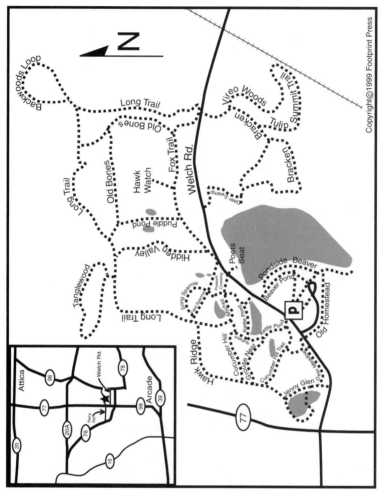

Beaver Meadow Nature Center

7.
Beaver Meadow Nature Center

Location:	1610 Welch Road, North Java, (southwest of Warsaw), Wyoming County
Directions:	From the New York State Thruway, follow Route 98 south. Turn right (W) on Perry Road, then left on Welsh Road. Follow the signs to the Nature Center parking area. Or, from Route 17, turn east on Welsh Road and follow the signs to the Nature Center parking area.

Alternative Parking: None
Hiking Time: A few minutes to 4 hours; your choice
Length: 7 miles of loop trails
Difficulty: 👣 👣 most trails, or 👣 Jenny Glen Boardwalk

Surface: Dirt trails
Trail Markings: Well-labeled by brown wooden signs with yellow lettering
Uses: 🚶 🎿 ♿
Dogs: Pets NOT allowed
Admission: A donation is requested ($2 per person or $5 per family)
Contact: Beaver Meadow Nature Center
Buffalo Audubon Society, Inc.
1610 Welch Road
North Java, NY 14113-9713
(716) 457-3228

Beaver Meadow Nature Center is a 324-acre wildlife preserve which has been developed by the Buffalo Audubon Society with walking trails, interpretive signs, and rest areas.

By the early 1900s, beavers were nearly extinct in New York State. A program of reintroduction was begun in the 1930s when beavers were released into Beaver Meadow Creek in Wyoming County. Today they thrive in the area. These furry animals engineered the ponds in Beaver Meadow Nature Center. They built dams using sticks and mud to impede the flow of a stream and form a pond deep enough for their home. Today the dam is camouflaged in places by vegetation. Two beaver lodges are visible near the dam. Beavers are nocturnal animals. They use their stick and mud homes to rest during the day. The best times to spot their heads as they swim across the pond are early morning and evening.

The Nature Center is an outdoor learning laboratory. The visitor center has seasonal exhibits, live animals, a discovery room, and a library. It is open year round, Tuesday through Saturday from 10:00 AM to 5:00 PM, and Sundays 1:00 PM to 5:00 PM. It is closed Mondays and major holidays.

A unique feature of Beaver Meadow Nature Center is the quarter mile long boardwalk with railings through a swamp area called "Jenny Glen Boardwalk." It is handicapped accessible, and allows people of all abilities to get close to nature and enjoy its beauty. The trail was named after the daughter of Western New York naturalist David Bigelow. Try a night hike along this boardwalk to hear the frog chorus.

This area is busy year-round. Hiking and nature discovery are typical summer pursuits. It's also the time of year when colorful winged insects flock to the butterfly garden. In the winter, snowshoes can be rented for a challenging romp along the trails. Maple sugar is made in the sugarhouse in early spring.

Many loops are available within this network of trails. Intersections are well labeled so you can create your own adventure by following the map. To find less heavily traveled areas, head back to the Long Trail, Tanglewood Trail, and Backwoods Loop Trail. Or wander south of Welch Road on Deer Swamp Trail, Bracken Trail, Tulip Summit Trail, and Vireo Woods Trail. The outside loop of this section south of Welch Road takes about 45 minutes if you walk briskly.

Campgrounds: Yogi Bear's Jellystone Park, 5204 Youngers Road, North Java, (716) 457-9644

Beaver Meadow Wilderness, Beaver Meadow Road, Java Center, (716) 457-3101

All of the trails tend to be hilly (2 boots) except the Jenny Glen Boardwalk (1 boot). Here's a short synopsis of what you'll find on each of the trails (listed alphabetically):

Backwoods Loop Trail – Follow the orange bands on the trees to stay on this less frequently traveled 10 minute loop through the woods.

Beaver Pond Trail – Stroll through the woods along the beaver pond. This trail takes you past a fern garden where various ferns are labeled. Here's where you learn about beavers. The trail leads you to a dead-end at the beaver dam and beaver house so you can actually reach out and touch them. There are interpretive signs about beavers, chipmunks, and wood-chucks along the way, and an observation platform overlooking the pond.

Chipmunk Run – This short connector trail has a chipped-wood trail base. It winds through the woods past hummingbird gardens.

Cucumber Hill Trail – Follow this leaf bed trail past a cross section of a 350-year old eastern hemlock tree and a set of outhouses.

Deer Meadow Trail – Follow this trail through the woods to circle an open grass meadow, then return to woods. An interpretive sign assists with bird identification along the way.

Deer Swamp Trail – A woods walk with switchbacks to a boardwalk through a swamp. The trail continues through the woods and along a pond.

Field Sparrow Trail – As the name implies, this is a walk through a field.

Fox Trail – Follow this mowed-grass path through a scrub field to the young arboretum. There is a spur trail to the hawk watch area.

Grouse Nest Trail – This trail is harder to follow than most as it winds through the woods. The adventurous are rewarded with an overlook to the kettle pond.

Hawk Ridge Trail – This woods wander takes about 5 minutes.

Hidden Valley Trail – Stroll on mowed grass through a young arbore-tum. There are several small loops mowed within the arboretum. This trail ventures through a small woods, then back to mowed grass in a valley between small hills.

Jenny Glen Boardwalk – A quarter mile of boardwalk with railings allows people of all abilities to experience the wetland and woods.

Kettle Pond Trail – Follow this chipped-wood path over two small wooden bridges and around a kettle pond with sea grasses and aquatic plants to explore. In spring you'll find families of ducklings on this pond. Kettle ponds such as this one were created when a large block of ice separated from the glacier. Water running off the glacier deposited gravel and debris all around the ice block. The block eventually melted, leaving behind a rough circular depression filled with water. An interpretive sign on this trail will help identify small aquatic animals.

Long Trail – This is a hilly walk on a ridge through the woods and along a mowed-grass trail through scrub apple trees. The entire trail takes about 30 minutes to walk. Along the way you'll cross some wooden bridges and boardwalks.

Mitchell Trail – Continue your meander on this pine needle and leaf trail. Cross a wooden bridge along the way.

Nuthatch Trail – This is a pine needle bed, connector trail through a pine forest. It has a bird observation area.

Old Bones Trail – This trail takes 20 minutes to walk through woods from Fox Trail to Puddle Pond Trail.

Old Woods Bracken Trail – Ramble through an old woods forest with a high canopy past lush fern beds.

Poet's Seat – A short walk down to a bench and pond view. Sit and reflect awhile.

Pondside Trail – This dirt path parallels the pond and goes to a lookout at a covered observation shelter. There are some steps along this hilly path.

Possum Crossing Trail – Stroll through the woods to a bench with a pond overlook. In spring the pond is lined with blue and yellow iris. You'll end at a young arboretum where an interpretive sign assists in leaf identification.

Puddle Pond Trail – For a short distance, follow the mowed-grass path through scrub apple trees. The area will open into field with the puddle pond (a pretty little pond) along the way. The trail also passes through the young arboretum.

Shadow Hill Trail – Wander through the woods with pine trees on one side of the trail and deciduous trees on the other. There are some steps to climb along the way.

Tanglewood Trail – Grouse are often flushed along this less frequently traveled 15 minute loop through the woods.

Tulip Summit Trail – Climb to a covered pavilion with benches; a mighty elevation of 150 feet. Nearby is a large tulip tree.

Vireo Woods Trail – Listen for the vireos as you wander these woods. You'll cross a wooden bridge over Grouse Brook and pass a cabin on your way to Welsh Road.

Date Hiked: _____
Notes:

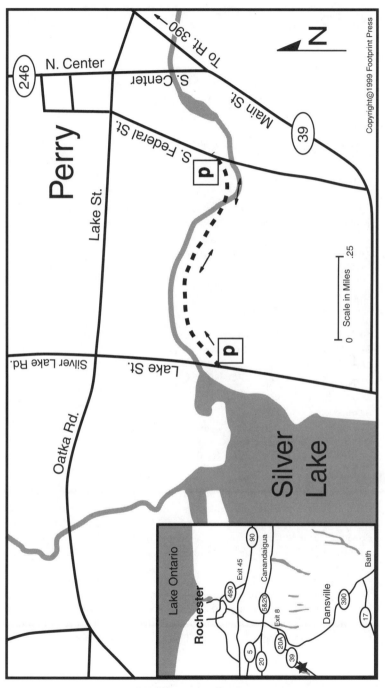

Silver Lake Outlet

8.
Silver Lake Outlet

Location:	Perry, north end of Silver Lake, Wyoming County
Directions:	Exit Route 390 at Geneseo (exit 8). Head west, passing though Geneseo, then turn west on Route 39. In the village of Perry, head west on Lake Street. Turn left to remain on Lake Street. (Continuing straight, the road turns into Oatka Road.) Cross over the outlet. The parking area is a dirt road south of the outlet.

Alternative Parking: South Federal Street parking area

Hiking Time:	20 minutes
Length:	0.8 mile round trip
Difficulty:	
Surface:	Dirt trail
Trail Markings:	None, but easy-to-follow
Uses:	
Dogs:	OK on leash
Admission:	Free
Contact:	Perry Development Committee 25 South Main Street Perry, NY 14530 (716) 237-4090

Silver Lake Outlet Trail is a short stroll on a dirt path which was once a railroad bed. A tree canopy will shade your way. In June the trail is lined with forget-me-nots and wild strawberries. The Silver Lake Outlet is a slow-flowing stream but it is a favorite of people who fish. The waters are alive with perch, bullhead, sunfish, northern pike, bass, crappie, and walleye.

As you hike, keep your eyes peeled for the Silver Lake sea serpent. In 1855 a group of fisherman spotted what was first thought to be a floating log. As it moved, they changed their description to that of a monster with a serpentine body and horrid-looking head. Over the next several months, numerous people claimed sightings. Observation towers were built along the shore and were manned by men known to be of good character. Expeditions were mounted to capture the beast, including one by a professional whaler. Business boomed at Perry's hotels and restaurants. Over time the sightings died away and life settled back to normal in Perry. There was some evidence that the serpent was a hoax perpetrated by the owner of a large Perry hotel called the Walker House. But townsfolk claim the sea serpent may just be hibernating, waiting for the right time to reappear.

Bed & Breakfast:	Perry B&B, 9 North Federal Street, Perry, (716) 237-6289
Campgrounds:	Woodstream Campsite, 5440 School Road, Gainsville, (716) 493-5643
	Zintel & Norris Campsite, 156 Lakeshore Drive, Castile, (716) 237-3080

Trail Directions
- Follow the dirt road toward a metal barricade and a sign saying "Perry Welcomes You to Silver Lake Trail."
- The outlet will appear on your left.
- Cross a wooden bridge over the outlet.
- Reach a parking area off South Federal Street.
- Turn around and retrace your path.

Date Hiked: _____

Notes:

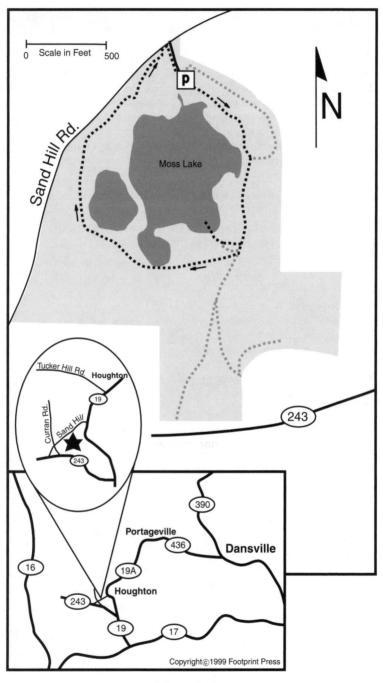

Moss Lake

9.
Moss Lake

Location:	Off Sand Hill Road, (southwest of Houghton), Allegany County
Directions:	Sand Hill Road runs between Routes 243 and 19, near where they intersect. A parking area is located down a short dirt road on the south side of Sand Hill Road. There is a sign for Moss Lake on Sand Hill Road.

Alternative Parking: None

Hiking Time:	20 minutes
Length:	0.7 mile loop
Difficulty:	👣 👣
Surface:	Dirt
Trail Markings:	None
Uses:	🚶
Dogs:	Pets NOT allowed
Admission:	Free
Contact:	Nature Conservancy Central & Western New York Chapter 339 East Avenue, Suite 300 Rochester, NY 14604 (716) 546-8030

Experience a living bog on your trip to Moss Lake. The Moss Lake bog became a registered natural landmark in 1973. This small pond has lilies floating on its surface and a boardwalk onto the bog where you can get a close-up look at carnivorous pitcher plants. Bend over to touch the moss and admire its cool moistness, like touching a wet sponge. A walk to the edge of the pond near the parking lot summons hundreds of 6- to 8-inch long catfish. As you approach, the waters come alive with squirming fish. There is a picnic table near the parking area.

Bogs such as this one began their life as glaciers retreated from the area. They left depressions, called glacial ponds, which filled with water from melting snow or rain. With no inlet or outflow of fresh water, the ponds then relied on rainwater for replenishment. Due to the low mineral content of melted ice and rainwater, these ponds were not attractive to the usual microscopic flora such as bacteria and fungi. Instead, the ponds were colonized by sphagnum mosses and heaths such as leatherleaf. The sphagnum moss consumed what minerals existed and excreted acids, producing acidic water. Over long periods of time, the moss built layers upon itself. The compressed moss formed a quaking mat over the water and became peat.

In a mature bog, the moss may cover almost all the water and become so thick that it can even support a person's weight. But walking on a bog is like walking on a wet sponge. Moss Lake is an evolving bog so it has only small sections of moss. Please stay on the boardwalks and do not step on the fragile moss.

Because the bog pond is replenished only by rainwater, it is low in oxygen. Add this to the low mineral content and acidity and you have a unique environment, one that is not enticing to most wildlife and one that supports rare species of plants. Bogs are home to carnivorous plants that trap and eat insects. These include the pitcher plant, sundew, and butterwort. They are also home to flowering orchids, water willow (a loosestrife), leatherleaf (an evergreen in the heath family), and wild cranberry plants. Most trees dislike the acidic conditions of the bog. The exception is the tamarack or larch, which can be found along the edges of the bog.

The peat from bogs was a precious commodity in years gone by. For centuries, northern Europeans dried the peat and burned it as fuel. It has twice the heating value of wood and two-thirds the heating value of coal. In World War I peat was used to wrap wounds because of its anti-bacterial properties and absorbency. It has also been used as diapers. Today people add sphagnum moss (peat) to soil for potting houseplants and landscape gardening because of its water retention properties.

Campground: Camping at Mariposa Ponds, 7632 Centerville Road, Houghton, (716) 567-4211

Trail Directions
• From the parking lot, head east on the dirt trail.
   [**Side Trip:** For a short, 10 minute loop, turn left before the wooden bridge. Bear left uphill toward the metal post with the orange top. The trail will loop back to the parking area.]

• For the main trail, continue over the wooden bridge.
• The trail takes you through a dense pine woods. Breathe in deeply the fresh pine aroma.
• Notice the boardwalk to the right. It takes you over the bog to the water's edge.
• At the "Y," bear right.
 [**Side Trip:** A left at the "Y" leads uphill to two paths, but neither is maintained. They eventually disappear into the woods.]
• Walk along the pond's edge.
• Emerge from the forest into grasses along the pond.
• Re-enter a young woods.
• The trail will parallel Sand Hill Road, between the road and the pond.
• The trail will bend left to avoid a wet area and lead to Sand Hill Road. Turn right, and then take an immediate right onto the preserve access road. Follow this back to the parking area.

Date Hiked: _____

Notes:

Rattlesnake Hill Wildlife Management Area

The Rattlesnake Hill Wildlife Management Area is a 5,100-acre tract of high elevation land. The land was purchased in the 1930s under the Federal Resettlement Administration when the depletion of farmland made farming the area unprofitable. The area was turned over to the Department of Environmental Conservation (D.E.C.) to be managed as a wildlife habitat.

Don't let the name of this area scare you away. Yes, there are timber rattlesnakes in the area, but they are shy creatures that stick to the more remote areas. If you stay on trails and roads, your chances of finding one are extremely remote.

As a wildlife management area, Rattlesnake Hill is open to hunting, so be sure to wear bright colors if you venture out during hunting season. The

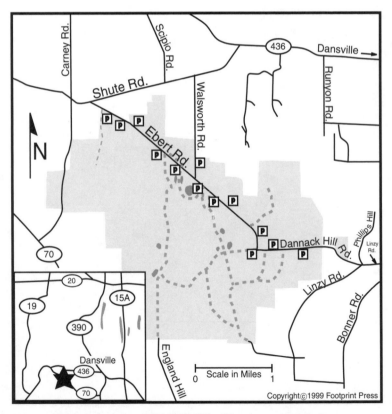

Rattlesnake Hill Wildlife Management Area

animals found here include white-tailed deer, wild turkey, ruffed grouse, gray squirrel, cottontail rabbit, snowshoe hare, mink, beaver, raccoon, and waterfowl.

This area has both natural and man-made ponds and several streams. Some of the larger ponds are stocked annually with trout. Sugar Creek, Hovey Brook, and Canaseraga Creek are known as trout waters.

Ebert Road is a seasonal road closed from November 15 to April 1. If you're heading out in the winter, Ebert Road becomes part of your trail. Camping is not allowed in Rattlesnake Hill Wildlife Management Area except by organized groups during non-hunting seasons by written permit from the Regional Wildlife Manager.

Bed & Breakfast: Kathleen's Country Estate B&B, 7989 Union
Corners Road, Dansville, (716) 658-4441

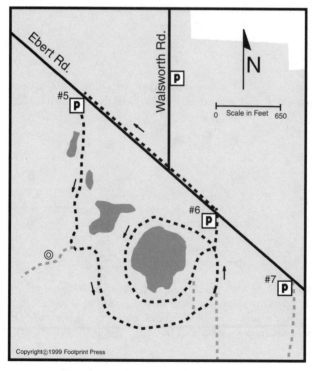

Copyright©1999 Footprint Press

Rattlesnake Hill - Short Hike   65

10.
Rattlesnake Hill – Short Hike

Location: Off Ebert Road, (west of Dansville), Livingston and Allegany Counties

Directions: From Route 54 East, turn right on Ebert Road. Park at the fifth parking area in front of a small wooden brown sign with yellow letters which says "trail." It's the last parking area before Walsworth Road. (Parking areas are not numbered – simply count as you pass them heading east from Route 54. Be sure to count parking areas on both sides of Ebert Road.)

Alternative Parking: The sixth parking area off Ebert Road, southeast of Walsworth Road

Hiking Time: 55 minutes

Length: 2 mile loop

Difficulty: 🥾🥾

Surface: 10-foot wide grass path (occasional maintenance)

Trail Markings: 2-inch round, yellow metal markers with black letters "trail marker"

Uses: 🚶 🥾 🐎

Dogs: OK on leash

Admission: Free

Contact: Regional Wildlife Manager
N.Y.S. Department of Environmental Conservation
6274 East Avon-Lima Road
Avon, New York 14414
(716) 226-2466
http://www.dec.state.ny.us

This short loop is on a grass trail. The grass can be high if it hasn't been mowed lately and the footing can be rough due to divots made by horse hooves. You'll pass three small ponds and one larger pond. The route includes a short, easy bushwhack through a mature woods.

Trail Directions
- From the parking area (#5), head south on the wide grass path through the woods.
- Pass a red metal gate.
- Pass a small pond on your right.
- Pass a second, then a third pond on your left.
- You'll come to a "T." Bear left, staying on the wide path and following the round yellow trail markers. (The trail to the right is orange-blazed but dead-ends. If you enjoy the challenge of following blazes, try this route. There often is not a discernible footpath so you have to rely on blazes alone. Be prepared to turn around and retrace your path at some point. We followed the blazes for 20 minutes before they ended.)
- Emerge from the woods to a pond and marshland area. Cross an intersecting trail.
- Bear left around the dike at the edge of the pond. At the southern end of the pond you'll have to bushwhack through the woods, but it's an easy bushwhack. Simply keep the pond on your left. It takes approximately 20 minutes to circumnavigate this pond.
- Heading north from the pond, you'll end at the sixth parking area.
- Turn left and follow Ebert Road for 5 minutes back to the fifth parking area.

Date Hiked: _____

Notes:

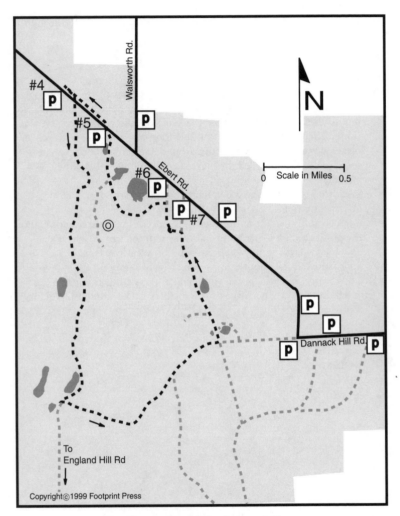

Rattlesnake Hill - Long Hike

11.
Rattlesnake Hill – Long Hike

Location: Off Ebert Road, (west of Dansville), Livingston and
                 Allegany Counties
Directions: From Route 54 East, turn right on Ebert Road. Park at
                 the fourth parking area. (Parking areas are not
                 numbered – simply count as you pass them heading
                 east from Route 54. Be sure to count parking areas on
                 both sides of Ebert Road.)
Alternative Parking: The seventh parking area, east of Walsworth Road,
                 near the wood storage shed
Hiking Time: 3 hours
Length: 5 mile loop
Difficulty: 👣 👣 👣

Surface: 10-foot-wide grass path (occasionally maintained) and
                 parallel dirt tracks in an abandoned roadbed
Trail Markings: 2-inch round, yellow metal markers with black letters
                 "trail marker" or "conservation ski trail" on some of
                 the trail
Uses: 🚶 🎿 🐎

Dogs: OK on leash
Admission: Free
Contact: Regional Wildlife Manager
                 N.Y.S. Department of Environmental Conservation
                 6274 East Avon-Lima Road
                 Avon, New York 14414
                 (716) 226-2466
                 http://www.dec.state.ny.us

Trail Directions
- From the parking area (#4), turn right on Ebert Road.
- In 25 yards, turn right onto the trail. Pass the yellow metal gate.
- There will be a long, gradual downhill.

69

- At 1.0 mile, pass a small pond on the right, then a few short uphills.
- Turn left at the trail junction. (A wooden storage shed will be on the right. A pond is beyond the shed. The path straight ahead continues to England Hill Road.)
- Now there's a long downhill. At first a stream will be on your left. Then you'll cross over it and the stream will dig a deep gorge on your right.
- Continue straight as a trail heads off to the right.
- Head uphill for 0.3 mile.
- At the top of the hill, turn left on the hiking trail and head downhill.
- Continue straight on a dam between two ponds. An outhouse is located here.
- Head between the outhouse and a large maple tree beyond the ponds.
- Re-enter the woods. A trail will head off to the left.
- Pass a pond on the right.
- Head down to a wet area.
- The trail will widen to a 10-foot wide grass path.
- Turn left at the trail junction. (Straight goes to a parking area (#7) and storage shed on Ebert Road.)
- Bear left at the next trail junction. (Right goes to the west side of a large pond, then to parking area #6 at Ebert Road.)
- Pass the orange-blazed trail off to the left.
- Pass two small ponds on the right, then a third on the left.
- At the parking area (#5), turn left and follow Ebert Road. Pass the trail you originally headed out on, then reach the fourth parking area.

Date Hiked: _____

Notes:

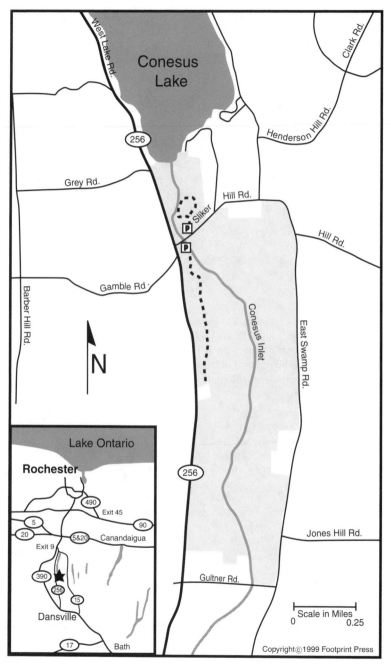

Conesus Inlet

12.
Conesus Inlet

Location:	At the southern end of Conesus Lake, Livingston County
Directions:	From Interstate 390 use exit 9 (Route 15). Head south to Route 256, then turn east on Sliker Hill Road. The parking area is on the south side of Sliker Hill Road, near the corner of Route 256.

Alternative Parking: Parking area on the north side of Sliker Hill Road

Hiking Time:	35 minutes
Length:	1 mile round trip
Difficulty:	
Surface:	10-foot wide mowed grass path
Trail Markings:	2.5-inch round, plastic D.E.C. trail markers
Uses:	
Dogs:	OK on leash
Admission:	Free
Contact:	N.Y.S. Department of Environmental Conservation 6274 East Avon-Lima Road Avon, NY 14414 (716) 226-2466 http://www.dec.state.ny.us

The Conesus Inlet Fish and Wildlife Management Area occupies over 1,120 acres of wetland in a valley floodplain at the south end of Conesus Lake. In the late 1960s, the New York State Department of Environmental Conservation (D.E.C.) purchased this land and initiated wildlife management programs to preserve and protect the vital wetland resource. An additional 83 acres were purchased in 1979 to provide access to Conesus Lake and to preserve a critical northern pike spawning habitat.

This walk takes you through woods along the wetland area. Bring a lunch and enjoy a picnic along the way. D.E.C. built a series of viewing platforms from which you're likely to see Canada geese, great blue heron, pheasants, ruffed grouse, and many other birds. Along the trail you'll also find evidence of muskrat, mink, raccoon, fox, and deer, which are abundant in the area.

Bed and Breakfast: Conesus Lake B&B, East Lake Road, Conesus, (800) 724-4841

Campgrounds: Conesus Lake Campground, 2202 East Lake Road, Conesus, (716) 346-5472

Southern Shores Campground, 5707 East Lake Road, Conesus, (716) 346-5482

Trail Directions
• From the parking area on the south side of Sliker Hill Road, follow the wood-lined gravel path to an earthen dam. The trail dead-ends, but this is a good viewing area.
• Backtrack and follow the hiking trail sign.
• Stop to enjoy the view from the three observation platforms on the left as you proceed down the trail.
• The mowed path will end at a small creek. Turn around and retrace your steps.

For an additional little hike, cross Sliker Hill Road. Pass a parking area and a yellow metal barrier. This trail is a short loop on a raised earthen berm through a marshy grassland area which is a pike spawning bed. The round trip will take about 15 minutes.

Date Hiked: _____

Notes:

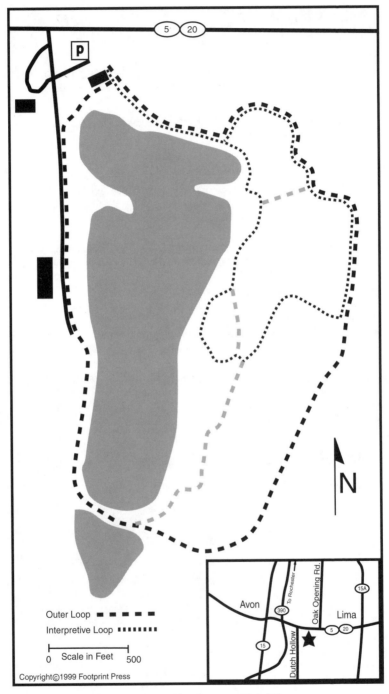

Twin Cedars Environmental Area

13.
Twin Cedars Environmental Area

Location: East Avon, Livingston County
Directions: On the south side of Route 5 & 20, east of Route 390.
                     Pull into D.E.C. Region 8 Headquarters. Bear left and
                     park in front of the red A-frame building.
Alternative Parking: None
Hiking Time: 35 minutes
Length: 1.0 mile loop
Difficulty: 👣 👣 👣
                     👣 👣 👣

Surface: Dirt and mowed grass trails
Trail Markings: Brown and yellow signs at some trail intersections
Uses: 🚶 🎿

Dogs: OK on leash
Admission: Free
Contact: N.Y.S. Department of Environmental Conservation
                     6274 East Avon-Lima Road
                     Avon, NY 14414
                     (716) 226-2466
                     http://www.dec.state.ny.us

Twin Cedars Environmental Area began in 1970 when D.E.C. purchased some farmland adjacent to its offices. In 1974, D.E.C. purchased another 59 acres and enlarged the pond. In the 1980s, the area was developed into an educational area, designed to emphasize the natural and man-made aspects of environmental conservation.

The A-frame building serves as an interpretive center. It is loaded with stuffed animals, an extensive collection of bird eggs, along with live fish and turtles. The exhibits and displays are designed to test visitors' environmental knowledge and stimulate their curiosity. It is open year-round, most weekdays from 8:00 AM until 4:30 PM. Call ahead to make sure the interpretive center is open to the public on the day of your visit. The trails are open any time.

Encircling the pond of Twin Cedars

The pond has been stocked with largemouth bass, black crappie, bluegills, pumpkinseeds, and tiger muskies. In 1993, triploid grass carp were added as a biological agent to control aquatic vegetation. Fishing is permitted with a valid license. Any triploid grass carp caught must be returned to the pond.

Two hiking options are described below. First is an outer loop – 1.0 mile in length. It circumnavigates the pond and takes you along the top of a high drumlin, or hill. The second loop is 0.7 mile long. This is an interpretive trail with numbered signs along the way. The numbers correspond to the trail guide listed below and help you understand the conservation practices in this environmental area. You can combine the two loops for a 1.7 mile hike (approximately an hour walk).

Interpretive numbered signs:

#1 Birds can benefit from man-made nesting structures. As you walk the trail, notice the purple martin "condos," bluebird houses, wood duck boxes, nesting rafts for geese, and nesting tripods for mallards.

#2 The dike you are standing on was built to impound naturally flowing water, creating this pond. The pond provides a suitable habitat for many amphibians, reptiles, birds, mammals, and fish that would not otherwise live here.

76

#3 This wet area is known as a seep spring, and some of the plants here are unique to this spot. Stepping off the trail could damage this fragile ecosystem.

#4 A clue to unseen moisture, the horsetail is the last surviving member of an ancient group of plants that once grew 40 feet tall.

#5 The pond shallows are rich in aquatic life because sunlight reaches all the way to the bottom. Look for a variety of plants, insects, reptiles, fish, birds, and mammals.

#6 Many of the trees and shrubs here were planted to provide food and cover for wildlife. Can you identify autumn olive, silky dogwood, highbush cranberry, and staghorn sumac?

#7 An area containing only one species of plant is called a monoculture. Notice how these white pines have been planted in rows. These "plantations" can be an effective way to raise timber, but lack the diversity to attract much wildlife. Although it provides shelter to some species, its food value is limited.

#8 This white oak provides a haven for many seedlings under its canopy. Notice the small oaks in the area that originated from this tree. Ground plants compete with the young oaks so only the strongest survive.

#9 Poison ivy! All parts of this plant are poisonous. It grows as a ground cover, an erect shrub, or a climbing vine. The white berries are eaten by 60 species of birds, but people who touch poison ivy run the risk of forming itchy blisters.

#10 This land was once covered by a glacier one mile thick. As the glacier retreated 15,000 to 20,000 years ago, rock and soil were deposited, forming the hill or drumlin you are standing on.

#11 The tall grass in front of you is switchgrass. It was planted to provide cover for pheasants. Pheasants need tall grass for nesting in spring and hiding from predators the rest of the year.

#12 The area to the left is mowed periodically to keep it in grass. The border between different cover types (water, grass, woods, etc.) is called "edge." Many animals are attracted to edges because they provide more food and shelter than a single cover type.

#13 Notice that several white cedar trees have fallen over. That's because a nearby spring makes water readily available near the surface so the roots do not need to go deep. As the tree gets older, a strong wind can blow it over.

#14 This shallow brook has an ecosystem quite different from the pond. What makes it different? What types of plants and animals in the pond would not be found in the stream?

| Bed & Breakfast: | Enchanted Rose Inn, 7479 Routes 5 & 20, East Bloomfield, (716) 657-6003 |
| Campground: | Bristol Woodlands Campground, South Hill Road, Bristol, (716) 396-1417 |

Trail Directions (1.0 mile outer loop, long, dark dashes on page 74 map)
- From the parking area, walk south in front of the A-frame building toward the pond.
- Bear left, walking on the mowed-grass dike along the pond.
- At the first junction, turn left to cross a small wooden bridge.
- Cross the culvert over a creek, heading uphill.
- Enter a short stretch of woods and pass cedar trees.
- A field will be to your left.
- At 0.2 mile, pass a trail to the right. Continue uphill into the shade of pine woods.
- Climb the steep drumlin.
- At the top you can rest on the bench and enjoy the views of farm fields to the left and the pond below on the right.
- Head downhill along the side of the drumlin.
- Continue straight, past stairs to the right at 0.3 mile.
- Enter woods, then a shrub field.
- Head downhill, continuing toward the ponds.
- Cross another dike, this time

A man-made nesting site in the Twin Cedars pond.

between two ponds.
- The trail bends right and follows the pond.
- At 0.8 mile, reach the D.E.C. maintenance buildings.
- Follow the road back to the parking area.

Trail Directions (0.7 mile interpretive loop, short dashes on page 74 map)
- From the parking area, walk south in front of the A-frame building toward the pond.
- Bear left, walking on the mowed-grass dike along the pond.
- Continue straight at the first junction.
- Cross a boardwalk.
- Pass a trail to the left. Notice the wild grapes and jewelweed along the trail.
- At 0.2 mile, turn right on Turtle Trail (left is the Woodchuck Trail).
- Cross a small bridge over a spring, then enter the woods.
- Enter a pine woods.
- Bear right at the "Y."
- Quickly reach a "T" and turn left on the Woodchuck Trail (right is the Blue Heron Trail).
- Climb stairs, turning left to the top of the drumlin.
- Pass a bench and head downhill, eventually to a pine woods.
- At 0.5 mile, continue straight past a trail to the left.
- Pass cedar trees.
- Cross over the creek culvert.
- Cross a small bridge.
- At 0.6 mile, turn right at the "T." The pond will be on your left.
- Walk the dike back to the parking area.

Date Hiked: _____

Notes:

Walks in Monroe, Ontario, & Yates Counties

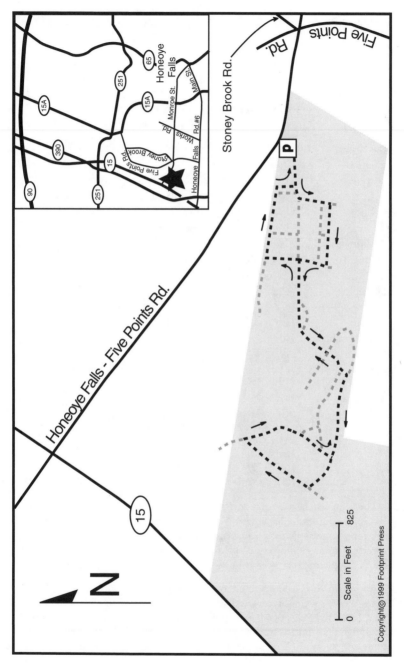

Quinn Oak Openings

14.

Quinn Oak Openings

Location:	Honeoye Falls-Five Points Road, Rush, Monroe County
Directions:	From Route 15 (south of Rochester), turn east on Honeoye Falls-Five Points Road. Watch for the Quinn Oak Openings parking area on the south side of Honeoye Falls-Five Points Road.

Additional Parking: None

Hiking Time:	45 minutes
Length:	1.5 mile loop
Difficulty:	👣 👣
Surface:	Dirt and mowed field trails
Trail Markings:	None
Uses:	🚶 🎿
Dogs:	OK
Admission:	Free
Contact:	N.Y.S. Department of Environmental Conservation – Forestry
	7291 Coon Road
	Bath, NY 14810
	(607) 776-2165 ext. 10
	http://www.dec.state.ny.us

The sign at the parking area reads "Quinn Oak Openings – Area of Exceptional Forest Character." We'll vouch for the exceptional character of the forests, grass fields, scrub brush fields, and swamps. This wonderfully diverse area is home to many birds, butterflies, animals, and over 400 species of plants. It's also a magical place for us humans to wander.

Approximately 4,000 years ago a major draught caused the demise of many native species of trees and allowed midwestern prairie plants to move east. It created fields of tall grass prairies surrounded by oak forests – an oak opening. The Indians noticed that these grass openings were havens from bugs and allowed them to get a broader view of approaching enemies so they kept the grasslands open with fire. The absence of trees in the oak openings made them easy targets for farmers. As white settlers moved in, many of the oak openings were put to use to raise crops.

Quinn Oak Openings is one of fewer than 20 oak openings remaining in the world. It was spared because limestone is only a few inches below the surface so it was hard to plow and virtually impossible to sink fence posts. This land was privately owned and was used to graze cows. The farmers continued periodic burnings to encourage grass growth. Today, D.E.C continues this practice to save this unique resource.

The trails can be a challenge to follow. They may be overgrown if it's been awhile since the last mowing or obscured by a blanket of leaves in fall. Sometimes the D.E.C. mows new channels through the grasslands, so the trails shown on the map may vary. Even so, this area is worth exploration. It's unlikely that you'll run into other humans. You're much more likely to scare up deer during your walk. Pay attention to the trees along the way. You'll find rare cinquapin oak and prickly ash. The grass is called indian grass and grows 6 to 7 feet tall. It's quite a sight in September at its full height with seed heads waving in the autumn breeze.

Bed & Breakfast: Greenwoods B&B Inn, 8136 Quayle Road, Honeoye, (800) 914-3559

Trail Directions
- Pass the blue metal gate as you head west on a wide, mowed-grass path. (You're not likely to notice the trails on the right.)
- Turn left (S) onto the first trail to the left. It will appear as a clearing comes into view.
- Take the second right (W) onto a 20-foot wide, uneven weedy swath. (Heading straight past this turnoff will land you in a swamp.)
- Pass a mowed trail to the right.
- Turn right at the "T," passing mowed strips.
- Cross a mowed grass area, then turn left (W) onto the main trail at 0.3 mile.
- At the "Y" you have a choice. Go left for high, dry ground. Bear right for level, potentially wet ground. The paths converge in a short distance.
- Stay on the main trail (two tire tracks) as it bends left.
- Pass an intersecting trail and cross a seasonal creek swale. Continue straight on the main path.
- Enter a young forest. (A small trail enters from the right, but we bet you

83

won't see it.)
- At 0.4 mile, turn right (W) at the "T" junction.
- Continue straight past a trail to the right. (This will be part of the return loop.)
- The trail will become rocky and hilly.
- Turn right (N) at the "T" junction.
- The trail bed returns to dirt and mowed grass.
- Turn right (SW) at the "T" junction to stay on the wide mowed path. (The path to the left dead-ends.)
- Bear right and pass a small trail to the left. (You can walk the small trail loops as shown on the map but they may not be maintained.)
- Pass a second small trail on the left.
- At 0.9 mile, turn left (E) at the "T" junction.
- At the next junction, turn left (NE). (The path bearing right loops through a 0.1-mile swampy area and should only be taken if the trails are dry.)
- Immediately pass a small, barely visible trail on your left.
- Continue past the seasonal stream and another trail junction. (This is where the 0.1-mile swampy loop returns.)
- At the "Y" junction, choose either option. A right will take you over high ground, left will be low ground. The paths converge in a short distance.
- At 1.2 mile, turn left (N) when you see a wide mowed area to your right.
- Turn right (E) at the "T" junction. (The trail to the left meanders to moss-covered rocks in a forest but dead-ends.)
- Pass several small trails to the right.
- The trail will bend sharply right (S) and meet the main trail.
- Turn left (E) onto the main trail for a short distance back to the parking area.

Date Hiked: _____
Notes:

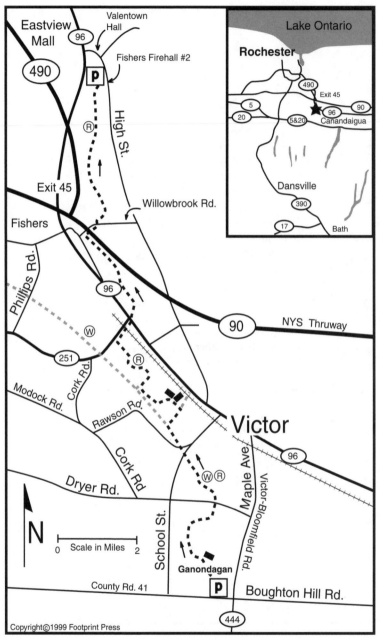

Seneca Trail

15.
Seneca Trail

Location:	Victor, Ontario County
Directions:	From New York State Thruway exit 45, head south on Route 96. In Victor, turn south on Maple Avenue (State Route 444). Turn west on Boughton Hill Road (County Road 41). The parking area for Ganondagan State Historic Site is on Boughton Hill Road, near the corner of Victor-Bloomfield Road (State Route 444).

Alternative Parking: Fishers Firehall on the south side of High Street, Victor (0.25 mile south of Valentown Museum).

Hiking Time:	3 hours
Length:	5.8 miles one way
Difficulty:	🥾 🥾 🥾
Surface:	Mowed-grass and dirt trails
Trail Markings:	Red blazes and diamond-shaped, red metal markers
Uses:	🚶
Dogs:	OK
Admission:	Free
Contact:	Victor Hiking Trails
	85 East Main Street
	Victor, NY 14564-1397
	(716) 234-8226
	http://www.ggw.org/freenet/v/vht/

This trail is steeped in history and is a wonder of diverse terrain. The journey begins at Ganondagan State Historic Site, once the home of a thriving seventeenth-century Seneca Indian village. Its downfall came in 1687 when the Marquis de Denonville, Governor General of New France, led an army of 3,000 men from Canada to massacre the Seneca in an effort to eliminate them as competitors in the international fur trade business.

In 1998 a replica Seneca Bark Longhouse was built on the site using red cedar, white cedar, and hickory. It was built with intimate attention to detail using information from oral, archaeological, and historical records.

Eventually the interior will be furnished with hundreds of reproduced Seneca and European artifacts from 300 years ago to help interpret the history of the fur trade in the late 1600s and the relationship between the Seneca and the European colonists. The village at Ganondagan is thought to have had more than 75 longhouses, housing as many as 3,000 people. Each longhouse housed up to 20 families. The replica longhouse is open Wednesday through Sunday, 9:30 AM until 12:00 PM and 1:00 PM until 4:00 PM.

Ganondagan State Historic Site also has a visitor center and Native American gift shop which is open Tuesday through Saturday from 10:00 AM until 5:00 PM. Ganondagan offers several loop hiking trails. For a detailed map, stop at the visitor center or see the book *Take A Hike! Family Walks in the Rochester Area.*

From Ganondagan, this trail winds through Victor, passing through Ambush Valley. In 1687 when the Marquis de Denonville and his soldiers came to Ganondagan, most of the Seneca warriors were in Illinois fighting the French. The few who remained attempted to ambush Denonville's army in this narrow valley, but they were significantly outnumbered.

Seneca Trail traverses wooded hills, crosses shrub fields, passes through wetlands, and follows two abandoned rail lines for part of its path. One was the Rochester and Auburn Railroad. The other was an electric trolley line which connected Rochester and Canandaigua before the advent of our interstate highway system. Much of Route 490 utilizes the old trolley bed. At one point along Seneca Trail, the hiker is treated to a view of the Rochester skyline in the distance.

Trail Directions
- From the Ganondagan parking area, head northwest across the grass toward the longhouse.
- Pass a brown and yellow "Trail of Peace" sign.
- Pass a perennial garden and the longhouse. The trail continues behind the silver and black "Ethnobotanical Trail" sign, west of the long house.
- Head downhill on steps.
- Cross a boardwalk.
- Pass a trail to the left. It's a short side trail to an interpretive sign.
- Cross another boardwalk.
- At an intersection, walk straight (N) where the orange trail signpost is

pointing.
- Bear right (N) at a "Y."
- Cross a boardwalk.
- At a trail junction, turn right (N) following the orange trail signpost, heading uphill.
- Emerge from the woods onto a mowed grass trail. Continue straight past a trail to the right.
- Pass a sign for "Meadow – Wood Fork."
- Re-enter the woods.
- At a "T," turn right (N).
- Pass a trail to the left, staying straight past a "Cottonwood Trail" sign.
- Climb a hill. Eventually a creek will be far below on your left.
- Watch for a trail junction and turn right onto the red-marked Seneca Trail. (The trail straight ahead dead-ends on a high point.)
- The terrain continues to be hilly.
- Exit the woods and walk through a shrub field.
- Re-enter the woods. Pass a large green and yellow "Hiking Trail" sign from Victor Hiking Trails. Head downhill.
- Cross a small wooden bridge and pass a trail to the left leading to private property. (Follow any signs carefully. This section of trail may be temporarily rerouted.)
- Cross Dryer Road. You've come 1.3 miles.
- Walk through a field, then cross a creek on a plank bridge.
- The vegetation becomes shrub field.
- At a swale cut in the hill, watch carefully for the trail to turn left into the woods. Head up to the top of the hill.
- Emerge into a shrub field and head downhill.
- At the base of the hill, turn left onto the abandoned Auburn railroad bed.
- Cross School Street.
- Cross Rawson Road.
- At the next junction, turn right (E) on a mowed-grass trail. (White-blazed Auburn Trail continues straight.)
- Enter the woods.
- Pass the historic village artifacts (also known as a dump) to your right.
- Watch for a trail to the left. Turn left (W). (Straight leads to Route 96 near BitsQuick Café. Not long ago this section of trail was under water, compliments of some industrious beavers. The beavers have moved on and the water level is once again low, allowing clear passage on the trail.)

- Pass abandoned metal and brick buildings on your right.
- Cross several bridges and boardwalks while passing through a wetland area.
- As you exit the woods, notice the horsetail on both sides of the trail. You're now walking on a raised strip which is the abandoned trolley bed. (If leaves are off the trees, you can see the Auburn trail running parallel to the left.)
- Cross logs over a stream.
- Reach a "T." Turn right and cross a wooden bridge. (Left connects to the Auburn Trail.)
- Cross a boardwalk and corduroy trail.
- Cross three wooden bridges. Watch for golf balls from Auburn Creek Golf between bridges 2 and 3.
- Emerge from the woods and cross a small wooden bridge.
- Turn left onto the driveway of Auburn Creek Golf.
- At Route 251, turn right.
- Cross Route 96, looking for the red marker on a post. You've come 3.7 miles.
- Follow the washed-out old dirt road uphill.
- Part way up the hill, turn left (NW) off the road. Cross a small stream.
- Pass conglomerate rocks, cross a farm road, and continue straight through a field.
- Pass a small trail to the right.
- Enter Ambush Valley. Watch for poison ivy. Head uphill at the end of the valley.
- Cross a gravel road (may be recently paved) and enter woods. Turn left (N) parallel to the Thruway.
- At Willowbrook Road, turn right (E) and walk through two road tunnels under the New York State Thruway.
- After the metal gates on the left, turn left at the green and yellow "Hiking Trail" sign and climb the hill.
- Bear right at a junction.
- Continue straight (N) through two mowed-grass trail intersections.
- Climb a long, gradual hill to a view of the Rochester skyline.
- Then a long downhill along the edge of the woods.
- Bear right as a small trail heads left.
- Climb steps and turn right along the edge of a yard.
- At the gravel road, turn right and cross grass to the firehall parking lot.

Date Hiked: _____
Notes:

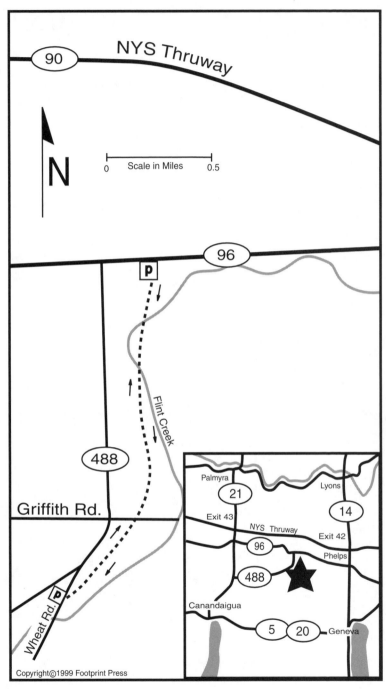

Ontario Pathways - Phelps

16.
Ontario Pathways – Phelps

Location: Between Phelps and Clifton Springs, Ontario County
Directions: From Phelps, head west on Route 96. The Ontario
                     Pathways parking area is on the south side of Route 96,
                     east of the Route 488 intersection. It is marked with a
                     wooden "Ontario Pathways Parking" sign.
Alternative Parking: Along the edge of Wheat Road (except from
                     November through April)
Hiking Time: 2 hours
Length: 3.4 mile round trip
Difficulty:

Surface: Mowed grass and crushed stone trail
Trail Markings: Some wooden signs
Uses:

Dogs: OK on leash
Admission: Free
Contact: Ontario Pathways
                     P.O. Box 996
                     Canandaigua, NY 14424
                     (716) 394-7968

The abandoned Sodus Point and Southern Railroad bed now has a tree canopy, making this a pleasant walk on a sunny day. You'll pass a small cascading waterfall in Flint Creek.

Ontario Pathways purchased this railroad bed in 1994. Since then volunteers have worked tirelessly to clear the trail and build the beautiful bridges you're about to cross. This rail line began service in 1873 as the Sodus Point and Southern Railroad carrying coal from the Pennsylvania mines to the port at Sodus Bay. By 1911, five million tons of coal were transported each year. Passenger service ran until 1935. A steam engine last traveled these tracks in 1957 and the last coal shipment occurred in 1967.

91

To read the full history and see pictures of the steam trains, stop at the kiosk in the parking area on Route 96.

Trail Directions
- From the parking area, head south on the grass trail.
- Cross Flint Creek on a wooden bridge.
- Pass old railroad bridge abutments, then cross Flint Creek again. Notice the cascading waterfall to the left. You've come 0.5 mile.
- Cross a smaller wooden bridge.
- Cross Griffith Road.
- At 1.7 mile, reach Wheat Road. Turn around and retrace your path back to the parking area.

Date Hiked: _____

Notes:

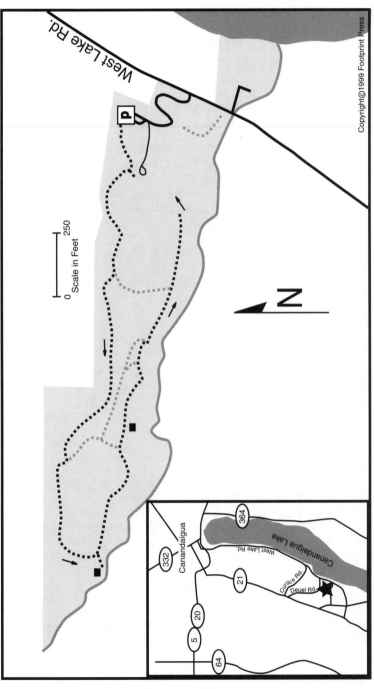

Onanda Park

17.
Onanda Park

Location: The west side of Canandaigua Lake, south of the city of
                    Canandaigua, Ontario County
Directions: West Lake Road, 7 miles south of Canandaigua, south
                    of Deuel Road. Enter the park on the west side of the
                    road, away from the lake. Follow the park road uphill
                    to the upper parking area.
Alternative Parking: None
Hiking Time: 45 minutes
Length: 1.2 mile loop
Difficulty: 👣 👣 👣

Surface: Dirt trails
Trail Markings: None but easy-to-follow
Uses: 🚶

Dogs: Pets NOT allowed
Admission: Free (on the west side of the park)
Contact: Onanda Park
                    West Lake Road
                    Canandaigua, NY 14424
                    (716) 394-0315

Onanda Park was first a YWCA camp dating from 1919, then Camp Good Days and Special Times which offered a respite to children with cancer. It became a public park in 1989 through a joint effort of New York State and the city of Canandaigua in an attempt to improve recreational opportunities and swimming access along Canandaigua Lake. Today the park covers 80 acres of land: 7 acres along the lake and 73 acres across West Lake Road, which is where you'll find the hiking trails.

Cabins, pavilions, and meeting facilities are available for rent within the park, mostly along the lakeshore. There are also a beach, fishing pier, picnic facilities, playgrounds, basketball, volleyball, and tennis courts on the lakeshore side. Admission is charged on the lakeshore side (free on the uphill side). The word Onanda derives from the Indian word for tall fir or pine tree, a symbol of simplicity and strength.

The trails wind up the hillside through the woods to observation platforms overlooking deep gorges and waterfalls that plummet over rock ledges.

Trail Directions
- Head uphill under the wooden sign "Upland Hiking Trail."
- At the first junction, a bench will be to your left. Straight ahead leads to cabins. Turn right (NW).
- At 0.2 mile, reach a "Y" and bear right. The trail continues uphill.
- Reach a "T" and turn right (NW).
- At 0.6 mile, the trail begins bending left.
- Continue bending left along a wooden fence. Reach hemlock overlook.
- At 0.7 mile, reach a "T". A short walk to the right takes you to a raised platform observation deck. A waterfall cascades down a mossy rock face into a deep gorge below. Toward the left is a view of Canandaigua Lake through the trees.
- Return from the platform. At the junction bear right, keeping the fence on your right.
- Soon a trail will head off to the left, but continue straight.
- The trail winds downhill.
- Reach a second observation platform at 0.9 mile. Here is a second water fall where the water slides down a smooth rock incline.
- The trail bends left.
- Quickly reach a "Y" and bear right.
- Quickly reach a "T" and turn right.
- At 1.0 mile, pass a trail to the left.
- Reach the mowed-grass area with cabins. Canandaigua Lake appears in front of you.
- Before the first cabin, turn left to re-enter the woods.
- Continue straight, heading downhill to the parking area.

Date Hiked: _____

Notes:

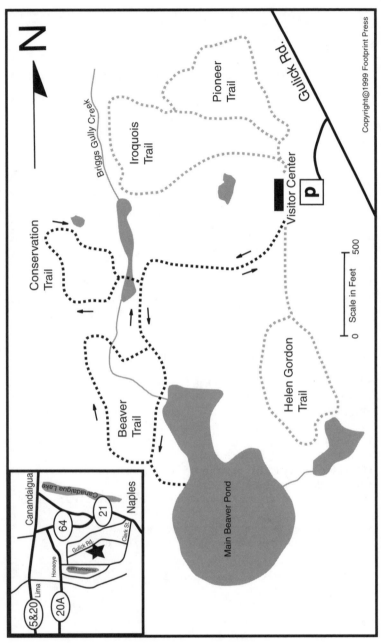

Cumming Nature Center

18.
Cumming Nature Center

Location:	Between Honeoye and Canandaigua Lakes, Ontario County
Directions:	From Route 20A in Honeoye, follow County Road 33 south to Pinewood Hill Road, then turn south on Gulick Road.
	From Naples, take Clark Street west to Gulick Road north.
Alternative Parking:	None
Hiking Time:	1 hour
Length:	1.6 mile loop
Difficulty:	👣 👣
Surface:	Dirt and sawdust lined trails
Trail Markings:	Well marked with signs at intersections
Uses:	🥾 🎿
Dogs:	Pets NOT allowed
Admission:	Adults $4, seniors (above 62) $3, students (K-12) $1.50, college students $3
Contact:	Rochester Museum & Science Center Cumming Nature Center 6472 Gulick Road Naples, NY 14512 (716) 374-6160

Cumming Nature Center is a 900-acre environmental education center and living museum operated by the Rochester Museum & Science Center. It contains a visitor center, beaver pond, hiking and cross-country skiing trails, a log cabin, a sugarhouse, and oxen. In the spring visitors can watch the sugarhouse in operation and taste the maple sugar with a pancake breakfast. Family activities are offered throughout the year including classes such as bird spotting, guided hiking, scarecrow making, and butterfly spotting. Festivals include a mushroom festival and fall harvest days.

The Nature Center is open Wednesday through Sunday from 9:00 AM until 5:00 PM. Trails close at 4:30 PM. It is closed from mid-November until the first week after Christmas, but then opens for cross-country skiing. The cross-country skiing trails are more extensive than the hiking trails, covering 15 miles of groomed trails. Ski rental is available for $8 a day.

There are five loop trails open for hiking:

Helen Gordon Trail is 0.75 mile long. It is an outdoor art gallery, displaying paintings of native wildlife.

The infamous pine tree lined trail into Cumming N.C.

Beaver Trail covers 1.5 miles with a walk to an observation tower overlooking a large pond, once the home of a beaver family.

Iroquois Trail is 0.6 mile long. Along it, paintings by Seneca artist Ernest Smith teach the culture and traditions of the Iroquois Indians.

Pioneer Trail takes you on a 0.75 mile walk past an 18th-century homestead and a sugarhouse where pure maple syrup is made each spring.

Conservation Trail covers 0.75 mile with interpretive signs along the way teaching a conservation ethic for our land and forests. The trail passes a working sawmill.

The walk we describe leaves the visitor center to loop the Conservation Trail, then proceeds to the Beaver Trail loop before heading back. In total it covers 1.6 miles. The trails are generally six feet wide, often sawdust-based and lined with boards. It is an easy-to-follow trail and soft on your feet. Along the way, large signs teach about forest management, ecology, nature, and the trees and animals that live in these woods.

Bed & Breakfasts: Greenwoods B&B Inn, 8136 Quayle Road,
Honeoye, (800) 914-3559

Acorn Inn B&B, 4508 Route 64, Bristol Center, (716) 229-2834

Naples Valley B&B, 7161 County Road 12, Naples, (800) 577-6331

Maxfield Inn B&B, 105 N. Main Street, Naples, (716) 374-2510

Landmark Retreat B&B, 6006 Route 21, South Bristol, (716) 396-2383

Nottingham Lodge B&B, 5741 Bristol Valley Road, Canandaigua, (716) 374-5355

Campground: Bristol Woodlands Campground, South Hill Road, Bristol, (716) 396-1417

The observation tower overlooking Beaver Pond

Trail Directions
- From the visitor center, follow the signs for Beaver Trail.
- Pass through a picnic area and proceed through a grove of red pine trees planted in 1930 in tidy rows.
- At 0.2 mile, reach a "Y" and bear right on Conservation Trail. Cross a bridge over Briggs Gully Creek.
- At the next "Y," bear left through a deciduous forest with a fern-covered floor.
- Reach an observation tower at 0.4 mile. Here's your chance to view the forest from tree canopy level.

- The trail bed becomes mowed grass.
- Cross a small peaked bridge.
- Pass some sitting areas along the trail – meditation time, anyone?
- At 0.6 mile, pass a small pond on the left.
- Reach the "Y" and continue straight.
- Cross the bridge over Briggs Gully Creek again.
- At the "T," turn right on Beaver Trail.
- The trail bed returns to a wood-lined, mulch bed.
- Cross a small bridge.
- Reach a "Y" at 0.8 mile. Go left toward Beaver Tower.

Robert Guthrie studies plant life along the boardwalk.

- Cross a boardwalk with a blind for observing swamp life and hummingbirds.
- Cross a small bridge.
- At the "T," turn left toward the Beaver Tower.
- Cross a short boardwalk.
- Follow the boardwalk out to the observation tower overlooking a lily-covered pond. The beavers have moved on but frogs and turtles abound.
- Retrace your path off the observation tower boardwalk and across another short boardwalk.
- At the first intersection, go straight toward the Nature Center.
- Cross five slippery bridges and boardwalks.
- Pass a small covered pavilion.
- At 1.4 miles, reach a "T" and turn left toward the Nature Center.
- Cross a small bridge.
- At the "Y," bear right.
- Walk through the pine woods and follow the path back to the Nature Center.

Date Hiked: _____

Notes:

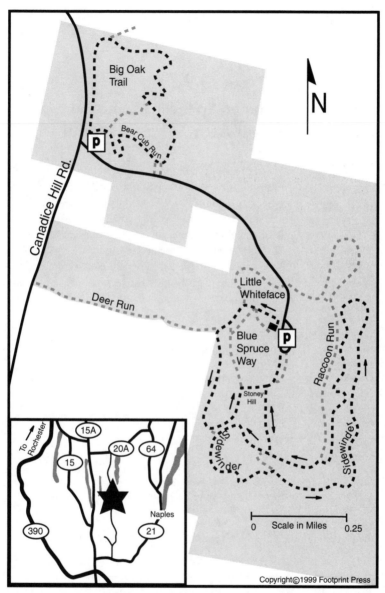

Harriet Hollister Spencer Memorial State Recreation Area
Big Oak and Sidewinder Trails

19.
Harriet Hollister Spencer Memorial State Recreation Area – Big Oak Trail

Location: South of Honeoye Lake, Ontario County
Directions: From Route 390, head east on Route 20A through
                 Livonia. Continue east past Route 15A. Turn south on
                 Canadice Hill Road. Pass Ross Road. Canadice Hill
                 Road will turn to gravel. Turn left at the sign "Harriet
                 Hollister Spencer Memorial Recreation Area." The
                 parking area is on the left near the park entrance.
Alternative Parking: In loop at end of the park road
Hiking Time: 30 minutes
Length: 1.9 mile loop
Difficulty: 👣 👣 👣

Surface: Dirt trail
Trail Markings: Some cross-country ski trail signs (blue squares) and
                 some trail-name signs
Uses: 🚶 🚴 🎿

Dogs: OK on leash
Admission: Free
Contact: N.Y.S. Office of Parks, Recreation
                    and Historic Preservation
                 Stony Brook State Park
                 10820 Route 36 South
                 Dansville, NY 14437
                 (716) 335-8111

High in the hills, between Canadice Lake and Honeoye Lake, this area is treasured by cross-country skiers because it often has snow when the surrounding area doesn't. The trails in this park are constructed, maintained, and groomed in winter by volunteers from the N.Y.S. Section 5 Ski League.

Big Oak Trail and Bear Cub Run ramble through deep woods and are shady and cool on a hot day.

Campground: Holiday Hill Campground, 7818 Marvin Hill Road, Springwater, (716) 669-2600

Trail Directions
- From the parking area, head north on the trail.
- Bear left on Big Oak Trail past a blue, "more difficult" cross-country ski sign. (Bear Cub Run is to the right.)
- Head downhill.
- Bear right at the "Y" to stay on the main trail.
- Cross a simple log bridge over a stream.
- Continue uphill. Notice the "1 km" sign on a tree to the right.
- Pass a trail to the right.
- The climb will get steeper.
- Toward the top of the hill, bear right, then take a quick right turn. You're now on Bear Cub Run. (Straight leads to the park road.)
- Pass a trail to the right.
- At the "T," turn left to the parking area.

Date Hiked: _____

Notes:

20.
Harriet Hollister Spencer Memorial State Recreation Area – Sidewinder Trail

Location: South of Honeoye Lake, Ontario County
Directions: From Route 390, head east on Route 20A through
                   Livonia. Continue east past Route 15A. Turn south on
                   Canadice Hill Road. Pass Ross Road. Canadice Hill
                   Road will turn to gravel. Turn left at the sign "Harriet
                   Hollister Spencer Memorial Recreation Area." Pass a
                   parking area on the left. The road will end in a loop.
                   Park along the road near the stone and wood lean-to.
Alternative Parking: The paved parking area at the park entrance
Hiking Time: 1.75 hour
Length: 3.3 miles loop
Difficulty: 🥾 🥾 🥾

Surface: Dirt trail
Trail Markings: Some cross-country ski trail signs (blue squares, black
                   diamonds) and some brown and yellow trail-name signs
Uses: 🚶 🚲 🎿

Dogs: OK on leash
Admission: Free
Contact: N.Y.S. Office of Parks, Recreation
                      and Historic Preservation
                   Stony Brook State Park
                   10820 Route 36 South
                   Dansville, NY 14437
                   (716) 335-8111

   High in the hills, between Canadice Lake and Honeoye Lake, this area is treasured by cross-country skiers because it often has snow when the surrounding area doesn't. The trails in this park are constructed, maintained, and groomed in winter by volunteers from the N.Y.S. Section 5 Ski League.

As you drive into Harriet Hollister Spencer Memorial State Recreation Area, you'll pass some metal guardrails on the left. Stop in this area to enjoy a grand view of Honeoye Lake in the valley. A bench labeled "a favorite place of Todd Ewers" is available to sit and savor the view. The park road is blocked during winter and becomes Overlook Trail – part of the cross-country ski network.

Within the woods you'll follow 8-foot wide dirt trails. Sometimes narrow trails veer off as shortcuts or deer paths, but stay on the wide trails.

The view of Honeoye Lake.

Campground: Holiday Hill Campground, 7818 Marvin Hill Road, Springwater, (716) 669-2600

Trail Directions (see map on page 101)
- Walk northwest with your back to the opening of the lean-to.
- Continue straight until the mowed area ends. Then turn left onto the dirt trail and head uphill.
- Continue straight past two trails to the left.
- At the "T," turn left and continue uphill. (Right is Little Whiteface Trail, which winds back to the park road.)
- At the "Y," bear right, uphill.
- Soon reach another "Y." Bear left (S). (Right is Deer Run Trail to Canadice Hill Road.)
- Pass a small trail to the left. Stay on the wide trail.
- Pass a small trail on the right. Stay on the wide trail.
- The trail will bend left.
- Reach a trail junction and turn right on Stony Hill Trail, heading downhill.
- At the next junction, turn right.
- Reach a "T" with a black diamond sign. Turn right.

105

- Bear left at a "Y" to stay on the wide trail. (To the right is a small, yellow-blazed connector trail.)
- Pass a caution sign as a long downhill begins.
- The trail sidewinds like a snake traveling through the forest.
- Several small trails cross the main trail.
- Bear right as the connector trail comes in from the left.
- Continue sidewinding on the wide trail.
- Eventually reach a "T" and turn left.
- At the next intersection (with a black diamond sign), turn right.
- Reach a "T" and follow the Raccoon Run sign, turning right.
- Bear left at the next junction.
- Follow the park road back to the lean-to.

Rich checks the map along the trail.

Date Hiked: _____

Notes:

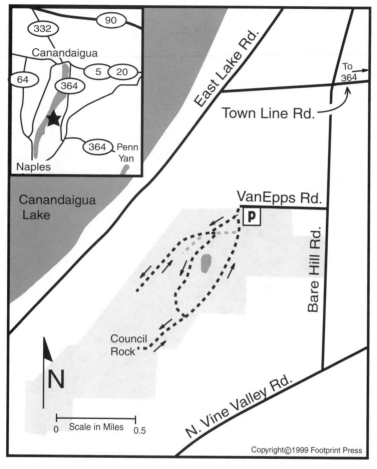

Bare Hill Unique Area

21.
Bare Hill Unique Area

Location: West side of Canandaigua Lake, Yates County

Directions: From Canandaigua, head south on Route 364. Turn
                     right (W) on Town Line Road, left (S) on Bare Hill
                     Road, and right (W) on Van Epps Road. Pass a brown
                     and yellow D.E.C. sign, "Bare Hill Unique Area." Park
                     along the side of Van Epps Road where it dead-ends.

Alternative Parking: None

Hiking Time: 1.75 hour

Length: 3.1 mile loop

Difficulty: 👞 👞 👞

Surface: Mowed field and gravel trail

Trail Markings: None

Uses: 🚶 🚴 🎿

Dogs: OK on leash

Admission: Free

Contact: N.Y.S. Department of Environmental
                       Conservation – Forestry
                     7291 Coon Road
                     Bath, NY 14810
                     (607) 776-2165 ext. 10
                     http://www.dec.state.ny.us

Bare Hill rises 865 feet above Canandaigua Lake and provides awe-inspiring views of the lake and valley. It also lives up to its name. The Department of Environmental Conservation mows around the trees on the summit, keeping this hilltop bare.

You will walk land where the Genundowa Festival of Lights originated. Genundowa was the name of a Seneca village near Bare Hill. Each year in early September, the Seneca Elders and the tribes Keepers would light a large fire on top of Bare Hill as part of the Seneca Autumn Ceremony of Thanksgiving for a successful harvest. This fire was followed by smaller fires along the lake, resulting in a ring of light as a gesture of Indian unity.

Seneca history is hidden in legend. One legend says that the first Seneca settlement occurred in Naples Valley around 1400. Other legends assert that they came from the Adirondack area or from Montreal, either following game or to escape warring tribes. In either case, by the 1600s the Seneca Nation numbered over 10,000.

Around 1570, five Seneca tribes united into the League of Five Nations, later called the Iroquois Confederacy. Historians call this early government the "greatest achievement of Stone Age man" because of its extensive code of laws. Council Rock at the summit of Bare Hill was the traditional site of the Seneca Indian council fires.

Trail Description
•From Van Epps Road, pass the yellow metal gate.
•Soon the trail branches at a "Y." A kiosk describes the history of the area. Bear right at the "Y."
•Bear right at a trail junction.
•Pass a trail on the left.
•At 0.7 mile, the trail dead-ends. Turn around and retrace your path.
•Continue straight through the first junction, then turn right at the second.
•A berm on your left contains a pond.
•Enter a tamarack forest.
•The trail bends left as you continue steeply uphill.
•At 1.8 miles reach a "T." Turn right.
•The trail dead-ends at Council Rock with a commanding view of Canandaigua Lake.
•Turn around and head down the hill.
•Pass a trail to the left.
•Pass a pond on your left.
•Pass another trail to the left, then the kiosk. Continue straight to Van Epps Road.

Date Hiked: _____
Notes:

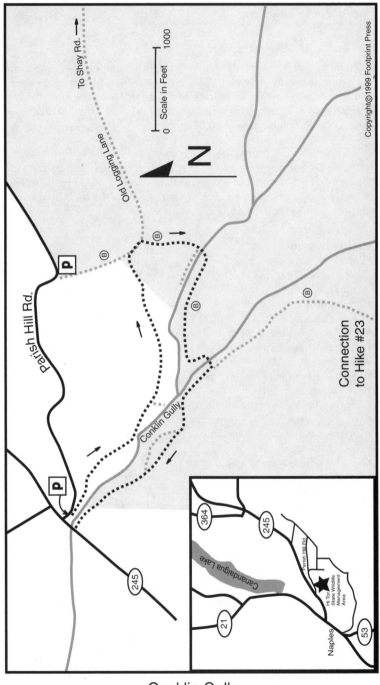

Conklin Gully

22.
Conklin Gully

Location:	Naples, (south end of Canandaigua Lake), Yates County
Directions:	From Route 21 (Main Street, Naples), turn east on Route 245. Turn right (E) on Parish Hill Road. Soon a small green and white D.E.C. "Public Hunting Grounds" sign will be on the right. Park along Parish Hill Road near this sign.
Alternative Parking:	A parking area to the right off Parish Hill Road, halfway up Hatch Hill.
Hiking Time:	1 hour
Length:	1.6 mile loop
Difficulty:	🥾 🥾 🥾 🥾
Surface:	Dirt trails
Trail Markings:	1/3 of the trail is blue-blazed, 2/3 has no markings
Uses:	🚶
Dogs:	OK on leash
Admission:	Free
Contact:	Hi Tor Wildlife Management Area N.Y.S. Department of Environmental Conservation 6274 East Avon-Lima Road Avon, NY 14414 (716) 226-2466 http://www.dec.state.ny.us

Letchworth does not have the only spectacular gorge in the Genesee Valley. Water rushing off Hatch Hill on its way to Naples Creek and Canandaigua Lake dug an equally spectacular, but smaller trench through the earth. Prepare to do some climbing to find it. This hike begins and ends with steep climbs. But the views of the gorge and waterfalls are well worth the climb. At the eastern end you'll cross two branches of the creek which merge to form the Conklin Gully gorge. The view draws you in but be wary. Don't go near the edges of the gorge – the banks often overhang with no support underneath. Because of this, Conklin Gully isn't the best hike for small children. There are no guardrails.

The hike is not to be missed. But consider taking along water shoes and seeing the gorge from water level after your walk. The rocks are slippery, so take care.

The cliffs of Conklin Gully

Camping is not allowed in Conklin Gully or the Hi Tor Wildlife Management Area except by organized groups during non-hunting seasons by written permit from the Regional Wildlife Manager.

Bed & Breakfasts: Maxfield Inn B&B, 105 N. Main Street, Naples, (716) 374-2510

Naples Valley B&B, 7161 County Road 12, Naples, (800) 577-6331

Vagabond Inn, 3300 Sliter Road, Naples, (716) 554-6271

Ice Cream: Bob N' Ruth's, corner of Routes 21 & 245, Naples, (716) 374-5122

Krystal's Café, 196 South Main Street, Naples, (716) 374-2319

Trail Directions
- From the pull-off area on Parish Hill Road, the trail begins 50 feet up the road (on the right-hand side). There are no signs marking this trailhead. It begins with a steep climb uphill (SE). The gully will be immediately on your right.
- Climb for 0.14 mile, then the trail levels out for a short distance.
- Continue southeast along the edge of the gorge. Notice the large pin oak trees clinging to the edge of the cliff.
- Climb again, then reach a lookout point.
- Enter a pine forest. A trail will head off to the right but continue straight, staying on the ridge.
- At 0.5 mile, meet the blue-blazed trail. Turn right (S) and begin following the blue blazes. (Left heads to the alternate parking area on Parish Hill Road.)

- Go 30 paces, turn right (W), and continue following the blue blazes.(The trail straight ahead goes to a parking area at the end of Shay Road.)
- Head downhill into the gorge.
- Reach water level at 0.6 mile. Ignore a trail to the right and cross the creek on stones.
- Continue following the blue blazes steeply uphill.
- Reach the best views of the gorge at 0.8 mile. Please stay away from the edges – they are not stable.
- Keep the gully to your right as you follow the blue blazes through the woods.
- The trail will bear left along a second branch of the creek with the water below to the right.
- At 0.9 mile, turn right and cross the second creek bed on rocks.
- Shortly, reach a "T" with a wide trail. Leave the blue trail at this point and turn right (NW).
  [The blue trail turns left and heads deeper into Hi Tor. Continue following the blue trail if you want to connect this hike with the Hi Tor Wildlife Management Area (hike #23) for a strenuous 6 mile loop.]
- Pass a clearing on your left. Continue straight into a pine woods.
- Conklin Gully is now on your right.
- Head downhill until the trail levels off.
- Reach a "Y." You can go in either direction. The trail to the left stays inland. The trail to the right follows the gorge rim. The two trails merge in 0.1 mile.
- Where the trails merge, it will be level for awhile.
- At 1.3 miles, begin a steep downhill. On the way down, be sure to notice the view of Canandaigua Lake to the right.
- At 1.6 miles, reach Route 245. Turn right, cross the bridge, then turn right on Parish Hill Road to return to the parking area.

Date Hiked: _____
Notes:

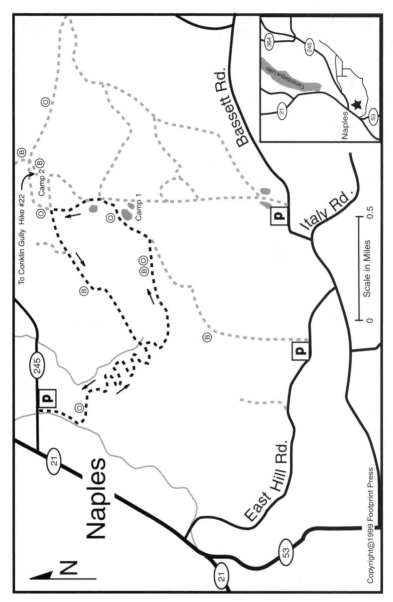

Hi Tor Wildlife Management Area

23.
Hi Tor Wildlife Management Area

Location: Naples, (south end of Canandaigua Lake), Ontario and
      Yates Counties

Directions: From Route 21 (Main Street, Naples), turn east on
      Route 245. After crossing the Naples Creek bridge,
      park on the right in front of D.E.C. near the sign
      "Naples Field Operations."

Alternative Parking: None

Hiking Time: 3 hours

Length: 4.5 mile loop

Difficulty: 👣 👣 👣 👣

Surface: Dirt trails

Trail Markings: 2/3 of the trail is orange-blazed, 1/3 is blue-blazed

Uses:

Dogs: OK on leash

Admission: Free

Contact: Hi Tor Wildlife Management Area
      N.Y.S. Department of Environmental Conservation
      6274 East Avon-Lima Road
      Avon, NY 14414
      (716) 226-2466
      http://www.dec.state.ny.us

      Finger Lakes Trail Conference
      P.O. Box 18048
      Rochester, NY 14618-0048
      (716) 288-7191
      http://www.fingerlakes.net/trailsystem

 Hi Tor (sometimes spelled High Tor) is an old English word meaning high, craggy hill or peak. You'll agree with the "high" part as you climb steeply up Hatch Hill. The crags are the sharp gullies and eroded cliffs which cross this hill, making it scenic and physically challenging.

115

The view of Canandaigua Lake from "camp 2."

This hike is in Hi Tor Wildlife Management Area, a complex of 6,100 acres of hills, woods, and marshlands managed by the Department of Environmental Conservation. The majority of the hike follows the Bristol Hills Branch of the Finger Lakes Trail (orange-blazed) as it crosses through Hi Tor, with a return loop on a blue-blazed trail.

The Bristol Hills Branch of the Finger Lakes Trail is a spur trail, which runs for 54 miles from Ontario County Park in the north until it meets the main Finger Lakes Trail at Mitchellsville (near the southern end of Keuka Lake). It makes a great five-day backpacking trip. The main Finger Lakes Trail runs for 557 miles between the Allegheny Mountains and the Catskill Mountains. Information and maps on all segments of the Finger Lakes Trail can be purchased from the Finger Lakes Trail Conference.

Prepare for a strenuous climb as you begin this hike. The trail switchbacks up Hatch Hill for 0.5 mile before following old logging roads on more level terrain. Most of the route is deep in the woods or under a tree canopy. A section on the blue-blazed trail is an old logging road which is wide and exposed to the sun. You have the option of continuing on the logging road (leaving the Finger Lakes Trail) for a short while on a side trip to a viewpoint, overlooking Canandaigua Lake in the valley far below.

You can also combine this trail with the Conklin Gully Trail (hike #22) for a strenuous 6 mile loop.

Camping is not allowed in Conklin Gully or the Hi Tor Wildlife Management Area except by organized groups during non-hunting seasons with a written permit from the D.E.C. Regional Wildlife Manager in Avon.

Bed & Breakfasts: Maxfield Inn B&B, 105 North Main Street, Naples, (716) 374-2510

Naples Valley B&B, 7161 County Road 12, Naples, (800) 577-6331

Vagabond Inn, 3300 Sliter Road, Naples (716) 554-6271

Ice Cream: Bob N' Ruth's, corner of Routes 21 & 245, Naples, (716) 374-5122

Krystal's Café, 196 S. Main Street, Naples, (716) 374-2319

Trail Directions
- From the D.E.C. parking area, head toward the brown kiosk next to Naples Creek. The trail begins on a grass swath along the east side of Naples Creek. Walk south on this orange-blazed grass path.
- At 0.4 mile, the trail bends left, heading away from the creek.
- Start the steep climb on switchbacks beginning at 0.5 mile.
- At 1.1 miles, reach the blue trail intersection. The blue trail will be your return loop. Continue uphill on the trail which is now blazed orange and blue.
- Reach a "T" where the blue trail veers off. (The blue trail heads south to a parking area on East Hill Road.) Turn left on the old logging road, following the orange blazes.
- Pass a man-made pond on the right. D.E.C. dug many ponds throughout Hi Tor as watering holes for the forest animals.
- At 2 miles, reach an intersection and turn left to stay on the orange-blazed trail. This old logging road continues to head downhill gradually.
- Pass a pond to the left, choked with cattails.
- At 2.1 miles, watch for brown posts on both sides of the trail. This flags the left turn of the Finger Lakes Trail into the woods. Turn left and follow the orange blazes into the woods.

117

[**Alternate Route:** If you want to reach a vista of Canandaigua Lake, continue on the logging road to where it takes a sharp bend left. This is the site of "camp 2" (camping is not allowed) and the vista. Return to the logging road and follow it as it bends left (W). It will pass the intersection of the orange trail and by continuing straight, you'll be on the blue-blazed return loop.

Or, by following the blue-blazed trail north out of camp 2, you can connect to Conklin Gully Trail #22.]

- You'll be going downhill through the woods on the orange blazed trail.
- At 2.3 miles, meet the logging road. At this point, leave the orange trail (which continues straight) and turn left onto the blue trail (the logging road) heading downhill.
- Pass another logging road to the right. It is a dead-end.
- The old logging road turns to a grass path. At 2.7 miles, the wide portion ends and the blue trail turns left into the woods.
- At 2.9 miles, cross a stream gully. Then up a short hill to a "T" with the orange trail. Turn right (NW) and follow the orange trail downhill to the parking area.
- Once back to your car face the D.E.C. buildings. The hill you're looking at is what you just climbed. Nice job!

Date Hiked: _____

Notes:

Hikes in Steuben
& Schuyler Counties

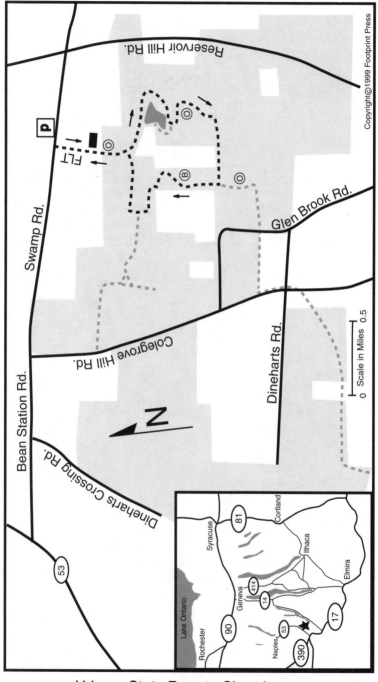

Urbana State Forest - Short Loop

24.
Urbana State Forest – Short Loop

Location:	Between Prattsburg and Hammondsport, Steuben County
Directions:	From the south end of Canandaigua Lake, take Route 53 south. South of Prattsburg, turn east on Bean Station Road. Pass Dineharts Crossing Road, then Colegrove Hill Road, both on the right. Watch for signs for the Finger Lakes Trail (FLT) on both sides of Bean Station Road (also called Swamp Road). The parking area is along Bean Station Road, just east of the trail crossing.

Alternative Parking: None

Hiking Time:	2.3 hours
Length:	4.8 mile loop
Difficulty:	👣 👣 👣
Surface:	Dirt trails
Trail Markings:	Orange and blue blazes
Uses:	🚶 🎿
Dogs:	OK
Admission:	Free
Contact:	Finger Lakes Trail Conference P.O. Box 18048 Rochester, NY 14618-0048 (716) 288-7191 http://www.fingerlakes.net/trailsystem
	N.Y.S. Department of Environmental Conservation – Forestry 7291 Coon Road Bath, NY 14810-9728 (607) 776-2165 ext. 10 http://www.dec.state.ny.us

Urbana State Forest sits on a plateau west of Keuka Lake. Your initial challenge will be to climb to the plateau. Once there, the hike is fairly level. In the 1800s this area was farmland. You'll walk some abandoned country lanes with larger roadside trees, plentiful apple trees, and rocks cleared from fields.

This trail has a special treat. It leads you around Huckleberry Bog, a rare occurrence at such a high elevation. Refer to the description of the Moss Lake Trail (hike #9) for more information on bogs. Huckleberry Bog supports high bush and low bush blueberries, and sphagnum moss, but no huckleberries. Huckleberry Bog is a misnomer that got applied to this area and stuck. High bush blueberries are the

Signs near the trailhead.

4 to 5 foot tall bushes that surround the observation deck overlooking the bog. Their berries are small but tasty. The less than one-foot tall bushes that carpet the forest, especially along the blue trail, are low bush blueberries. These berries are tasty too, but even smaller.

Another rare treat is the Nature Trail Guide, which was produced by trail maintainer Irene Szabo. This 32-page booklet can be picked up at two locations along the trail. It describes the trees, plants, and farm remnants found along the way. Your walk can become a free nature study and a full day adventure, thanks to Irene's great efforts. Please return the guide after using so it will be available for the next nature lover.

This trail is well blazed. You'll follow orange blazes for the first half and blue blazes for most of the return. The trail will wind on and off the country lanes and forest paths, so follow the blazes carefully.

Camping: Allowed in Urbana State Forest. For stays of three days or longer, or by groups of 10 or more, obtain a free camping permit from the D.E.C. Regional Ranger at the address above.

Trail Directions
- From the parking area along Bean Station Road, head across the road (SW) to the FLT trail crossing.
- At the yellow FLT signs, turn left, crossing a small wooden bridge, onto the trail. Begin following orange blazes.
- Pass Covell Cemetery and continue uphill following the blazes.
- Pass Evangeline shelter.
- Pass a wire barricade as you leave private property.
- At 0.7 mile, reach the junction with the blue trail. (This will be your return loop.) Continue straight following orange blazes.
- The trail will wind on and off an old woods lane. Follow orange blazes carefully.
- At 1.4 miles the trail turns right (S).
- Pass a small deck overlooking the bog.
- At 1.6 miles a blue spur trail (0.15-mile long) will be on the right. (It leads part way around the bog.) Bear left staying on the orange-blazed trail.
- Cross a country lane.
- At 2.6 miles, cross a stream, then reach the blue-blazed trail and turn right (N), following blue blazes.
- The blue blazed trail will follow old country lanes and wind through the woods.
- At 2.9 miles, turn right onto an old road.
- At 3.5 miles, an unblazed lane heads off to the left and the blue trail bends right. (This lane is part of the Urbana State Forest – Long Loop Trail #25).
- At 4.0 miles, reach the orange-blazed trail intersection and turn left.
- Follow the orange blazes downhill to Bean Station Road.

Date Hiked: _____
Notes:

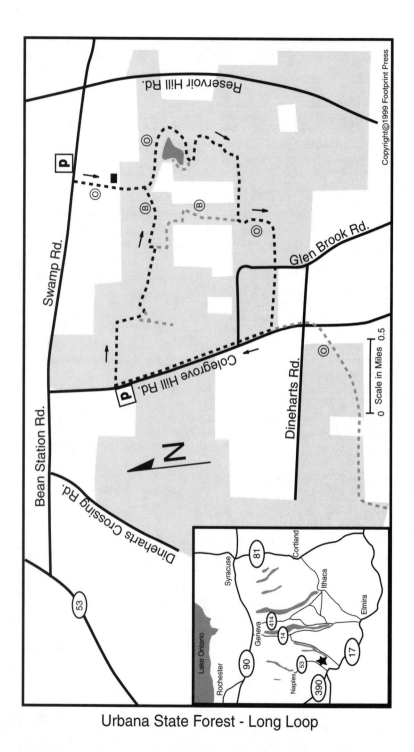

Urbana State Forest - Long Loop

25.
Urbana State Forest – Long Loop

Location:	Between Prattsburg and Hammondsport, Steuben County
Directions:	From the south end of Canandaigua Lake, take Route 53 south. South of Prattsburg, turn east on Bean Station Road. Pass Dineharts Crossing Road, then Colegrove Hill Road, both on the right. Watch for signs for the Finger Lakes Trail (FLT) on both sides of Bean Station Road (also called Swamp Road). The parking area is along Bean Station Road, just east of the trail crossing.
Alternative Parking:	A parking area on Colegrove Hill Road, across from abandoned Bog Road.
Hiking Time:	3.75 hours
Length:	7.1 mile loop
Difficulty:	🥾 🥾 🥾
Surface:	Dirt trails
Trail Markings:	Orange and blue blazes
Uses:	🚶
Dogs:	OK
Admission:	Free
Contact:	Finger Lakes Trail Conference P.O. Box 18048 Rochester, NY 14618-0048 (716) 288-7191 http://www.fingerlakes.net/trailsystem
	N.Y.S. Department of Environmental Conservation – Forestry 7291 Coon Road Bath, NY 14810-9728 (607) 776-2165 ext. 10 http://www.dec.state.ny.us

This trail shows all the features of the Urbana State Forest (see hike #24) in a longer hike. In the 1800s, this area was farmland. One of the country lanes you'll walk, called Bog Road, disappeared from maps in the 1930s. Notice the larger roadside trees, plentiful apple trees, and rocks cleared from fields as you walk the old lanes.

The walk includes a 1.3-mile stretch of road, but the road is a one-lane seasonal dirt road which is pleasant to walk. We saw a coyote scoot across as we walked this road. It also offers a panoramic view of the muckland in a side valley off Prattsburg's north-south valley, toward Kanona and the Cohocton River.

A white blaze points the way along the FLT.

Trail Directions
- From the parking area along Bean Station Road, head across the road (SW) to the FLT trail crossing.
- At the yellow FLT signs, turn left, crossing a small wooden bridge, onto the trail. Begin following orange blazes.
- Pass Covell Cemetery and continue uphill following the blazes.
- Pass Evangeline shelter.
- Pass a wire barricade as you leave private property.
- At 0.7 mile, reach the junction with the blue trail coming in from the right. (This will be your return loop.) Continue straight following orange blazes.
- The trail will wind on and off an old woods lane. Follow orange blazes carefully.
- At 1.4 miles, the trail turns right (S).
- Pass a small deck overlooking the bog.
- At 1.6 miles, a blue spur trail (0.15-mile long) will be on the right. (It leads part way around the bog.) Bear left following orange blazes.
- Pass the hugging trees. The entwined oak and hemlock trees are over

126

100 years old.
- Cross a country lane.
- At 2.6 miles, cross a stream, then reach the blue-blazed trail to the right. Turn left (S) staying on the orange trail.
- At 2.9 miles, emerge to a shrub field.
- Cross Glen Brook Road at 3.1 miles.
- Cross three streambeds, then head uphill.
- Reach Colegrove Hill Road at 3.5 miles. Turn right and walk along this seasonal dirt road for 1.3 miles.
- Eventually the road will head steadily downhill with a view of the Prattsburg valley. At the next bend, turn right (E) onto the gravel lane (abandoned Bog Road which is not blazed).
- Reach a "Y" and bear left.
- Quickly reach a "T" and turn left.
- At 5.8 miles reach a "T" with the blue-blazed trail. Turn left and follow the blue blazes.
- Meet the orange-blazed trail and turn left.
- Follow the orange blazes downhill to Bean Station Road.

Date Hiked: _____

Notes:

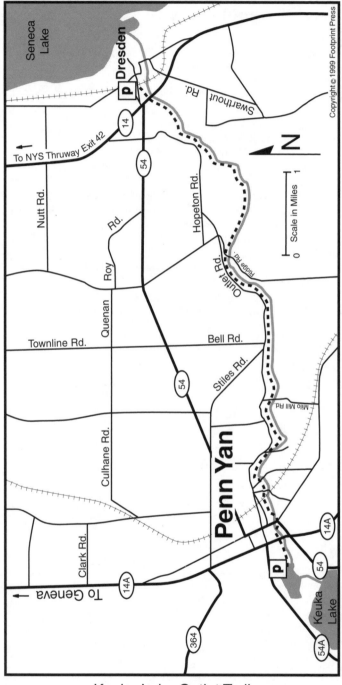

Keuka Lake Outlet Trail

26.
Keuka Lake Outlet Trail

Location: Dresden to Penn Yan, Yates County
Directions: From Route 14 south along the west side of Seneca
                 Lake, turn left (E) at Route 54 heading toward Main
                 Street, Dresden. There is a Citgo gas station and the
                 Crossroads Ice Cream Shop at the corner. At the
                 Crossroads Ice Cream Shop, take an immediate right
                 onto Seneca Street. Parking is on your right just before
                 the railroad tracks.
Alternative Parking: Penn Yan, Marsh Development Project, Little League
                 Baseball, on Route 54A (Elm Street)
Hiking Time: 4 hours
Length: 7.5 miles one way
Difficulty: 🥾 🥾
                 🥾 🥾

Surface: Dirt (western end is paved)
Trail Markings: Green and white metal "Trail" signs
Uses: 🚶 🚴 🎿 🐎 🛷

Dogs: OK on leash
Admission: Free
Contact: Friends of the Finger Lakes Outlet
                 P.O. Box 231
                 Penn Yan, NY 14527

The strip of land you will be walking from Seneca Lake to Keuka Lake is steeped in history. You'll see evidence of places and events from several bygone eras as you walk westward.

In the middle of the nineteenth century, two fingers of water connected the 274-foot drop between Keuka and Seneca Lakes, the outlet to power mills, and the Crooked Lake Canal for boat traffic. A dam and guardhouse in Penn Yan controlled the water flow to both. The outlet, which still carries water from one lake to the next, was formed by a ground fault in the Tully limestone allowing water to run between the two lakes. Along its

129

banks, you'll see remnants of the many mills which once harnessed the waterpower.

The first white settlers arrived in this area around 1788, attracted by the reliable water source at the outlet. In 1789 Seneca Mill was built along the raging waters of Keuka Lake outlet to grind flour with a 26-foot, overshot flywheel. From then until 1827, a small religious group called the Society of Universal Friends built 12 dams and many mills that helped make the area a thriving community. The mills and shops produced flour (gristmills), lumber (sawmills), tool handles, linseed oil, plaster, and liquor (distilleries). There were two triphammer forges, eight fulling and carding mills, tanneries, and weavers making cotton and wool cloth. By 1835, 30 to 40 mills were in operation. But, by 1900, only five mills remained, mainly making paper from straw. The last water-turbine mill ceased operation in 1968.

A waterfall that was once dammed for a mill site along Keuka Lake Outlet.

In 1833 New York State opened the Crooked Lake Canal to span the six miles between the two lakes and move farm products to eastern markets. The canal was four feet deep and had 28 wooden locks. It took a vessel six hours to journey through the canal. As business boomed in the mills, the state widened and deepened the canal and replaced the wooden locks with stone. But the canal lost money every year of its 44-year history, so in 1877 the state auctioned off all the machinery and stone. Only the towpath remained. In 1844 a railroad was built on the towpath. Initially operated by the Penn Yan and New York Railway Company, it eventually became part of the New York Central System. Railway men called it the "Corkscrew Railway" because of its countless twists and turns. The line operated until 1972 when the tracks were washed out by the flood from Hurricane Agnes.

A local group interested in recreational use of the ravine convinced the town of Penn Yan to buy the property in 1981. Since then, it has been developed and maintained by a volunteer group called the Friends of the Outlet. Trail signs and outhouses were recently added along the route.

Reference Guides: Purchase an illustrated guide to the Keuka Lake Outlet for $1.00 from the Yates County Historian, 110 Court Street, Penn Yan, NY 14527. A packet of information on the history of the mill sites, canal, and railroad of the Keuka Lake Outlet is available for $3.00 at stores in Penn Yan.

Bed & Breakfasts:	Finton's Landing B&B, 661 East Lake Road, Penn Yan, (315) 536-3146
	Fox Inn, 158 Main Street, Penn Yan, (800) 901-7997
	Keuka Overlook, 5777 Old Bath Road, Dundee, (607) 292-6877
	Merrit Hill Manor, 2756 Coates Road, Penn Yan, (315) 536-7682
	Trimmer House B&B, 145 East Main Street, Penn Yan, (800) 968-8735
	Tudor Hall B&B, 762 East Bluff Drive, Penn Yan, (315) 536-9962
	The Wagener Estate, 351 Elm Street, Penn Yan, (315) 536-4591
Ice Cream:	Crossroads Ice Cream Shop, Dresden, (315) 531-5311
Campground:	Wigwam Keuka Lake Campground, 3324 Esperanza Road, Bluff Point, (315) 536-6352

Trail Directions
• The trail leads downhill from the back-right corner of the Dresden

131

parking lot, heading west.
- Cross under the Route 14 bridge. The land you're on used to be the Dresden Mill Pond.
- The wetland to your right (north of the trail) is the old Crooked Lake Canal.
- Cross two wooden bridges.
- Notice the steep cliffs on both sides. Where the canal and outlet are close together was the location of Lock 3. Watch for the cement and rebar millstone.
- Cross a dirt road. This was Hopeton Road, which in the 1790s connected Geneva to Bath through the town of Hopeton. To your left you can still see remnants of the iron-pony, truss bridge over the outlet. The bridge was built in 1840 and rests on stone abutments. This area was once a community of mills. Hopeton Grist Mill was located just beyond the dirt road on the left. Nothing remains of it today.
- On your left is a pleasant rest area with large rocks where you can sit along the water.
- Across the outlet, Bruces Gully cascades water over three waterfalls to join the outlet. Eventually the Friends of the Outlet plan to build a hiking trail through the gully. The dark gray rock, which peels in thin layers, is Genesee shale.
- Pass a cement pillar on your right. The big "W" on the pillar signaled the train conductor to blow his whistle.
- At the two-mile point are the remains of the J.T. Baker Chemical Company, manufacturers of the pesticide carbine bisulfide until 1968. At one time, this was also the site of a gristmill and several paper mills.
- Here you'll see your first waterfall. The top step of the falls was the old dam, constructed in 1827 and the last of the 12 dams built along the outlet. Both Cascade Mill and Mallory's Mill used the water that was held back by this dam.
- Follow the wide gravel path through the building area.
- Pass old Kelly Tire buildings. The Friends of the Outlet recently renovated these buildings into the Alfred Jensen Memorial Visitor Center. It's a good place to stop if you need a restroom.
- Follow the green and white trail signs as the trail branches to the left.
- At 2.6 miles, cross the paved Ridge Road. In 1805 May's Mills stood at this site. It had a gristmill, a sawmill, and a post office. In the 1820s this area was home to a cotton factory, then a distillery.

- Continue along the outlet. Outlet Road parallels close to the trail.
- Just over a culvert is another cement post displaying a "W," then another cement marker with "D3" which told the conductor that Dresden was three miles away. This means that you're almost halfway to Penn Yan.
- Pass a parking lot off Outlet Road. The brick remnants on the right were once a factory that turned rags into paper.
- Look for the large rock between the trail and the outlet. A plaque on the side facing the outlet commemorates John Sheridan, a lawyer who negotiated the purchase of land for the Keuka Lake Outlet Preservation Area. The stone remnants across the outlet were once a forge. At one time a road crossed over the dam at this spot. Seneca Mill, the first mill site, was located at this falls, the largest falls on the outlet.
- On your right (away from the outlet) is a stone wall with a large round opening. This used to house a pipe to vent train smoke out of the valley.
- The machinery that remains at the top of the dam controlled water flow through a sluiceway. The original Friends Mill, a complex of paper and gristmills, was here.
- The trail bears right through Lock 17, which was the downstream end of

The trail now passes through Lock 17 of the Crooked Lake Canal.

a series of four locks needed to maneuver the elevation drop.

- You're now walking in a ravine of the old canal bed. In May this segment of trail is lined with trillium. It's also an active beaver area.
- Pass another cement whistle sign on the right.
- The cement wall in the water is the end of a race from Milo Mills. The stagnant water on the left is the raceway. From here to Penn Yan was the most industrialized section of the outlet.
- A large brick chimney towers over the remains of a paper mill, built in 1890, burned in 1910, and then rebuilt. You can still see the 17-foot flywheel which used two miles of hemp cable and was run by a steam engine. The machinery was manufactured at the Rochester foundry at Brown's Race.
- At 4.4 miles, cross Milo Mill Road.
- Cross a bridge over a wood-lined sluice. This used to carry water to Shutt's Mill, which dates back to about 1850.
- A small side path immediately to the left leads to the ruins of Shutt's Mill. You can still see the stone vats from this paper mill which manufactured wallboard. Shutt's Mill burned in 1933. The first mill at this site was a sawmill built in 1812. It was followed by a wool mill, a gristmill, and a fulling mill. Beware of the poison ivy in the area.
- The waterfall on the far side of the outlet, just before a road and bridge, is outflow from the municipal sewage plant.
- Cross a road. Dibbles Mill used to make wooden wheels in this area.
- The green shed across the road on the right was a blacksmith shop from canal times (around 1838). The blacksmith specialized in shoeing mules.
- At 5.5 miles, cross paved Fox Mill Road. If you take a left on Fox Mill Road, then a quick right toward the outlet, you'll find remains from the Fox Mill which manufactured straw paper. The stone for the walls was moved here from the dismantled locks of Crooked Lake Canal around 1865.
- Pass a sign for St. John's Mill. Other than the sign, there's nothing to see. The mill used to be across the outlet.
- Cross paved Cherry Street.
- The trail becomes paved.
- Pass under a railroad trestle called "High Bridge." It was originally built of wood in 1850 and was rebuilt in 1890.
- The large circular hollow just after the trestle was once a turntable for the train.

134

- Pass signs for an exercise trail. After the chin-up bars on the right, a small path leads left to another cement railroad marker "D6," indicating six miles from Dresden.
- Reach the wooden bridge which served as a railroad trestle to Birkett Mills in 1824. Birkett Mills took their water turbines out in 1947.
- At 6.5 miles, pass under the Main Street (Penn Yan) bridge which was built in 1884 from canal stone. This area used to have the guardhouse for the canal. The dam on the right is used to control water level in Keuka Lake. The brown building you can see was a grain warehouse. At one time this section of trail was home to several woodworking factories, a cooperage, and a sash-and-blind factory.
- Pass through a park.
- Cross the pedestrian bridge over the outlet.
- Continue through Penn Yan Recreation Complex on the paved path. You pass restrooms, a boat launch, tennis courts, and a small play ground.
- Cross another wooden bridge over Sucker Brook.
- Pass through the athletic fields to the parking lot in Marsh Development Project on Route 54A.

Date Hiked: _____
Notes:

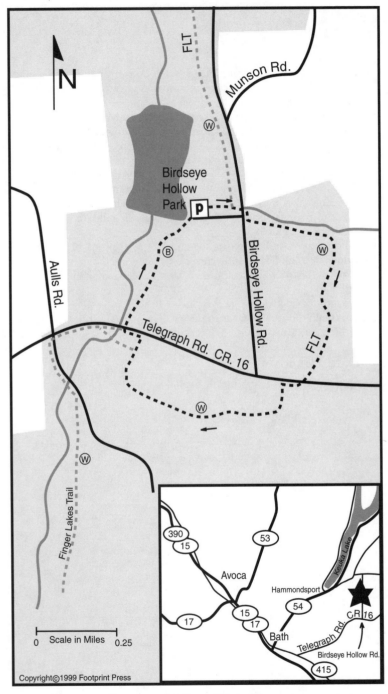

Birdseye Hollow State Forest

27.

Birdseye Hollow State Forest

Location: Southeast of Keuka Lake, Steuben County

Directions: From Bath, follow Route 415 east, then County Route
                      16 (Telegraph Road) east. Turn left (N) onto Birdseye
                      Hollow Road. Birdseye Hollow County Park will be
                      0.4 mile north, on the left.

Alternative Parking: None

Hiking Time: 1.0 hour

Length: 2.0 mile loop

Difficulty: 🥾 🥾
                      🥾 🥾

Surface: Dirt trails

Trail Markings: White and blue blazes

Uses: 🚶

Dogs: OK on leash

Admission: Free

Contact: Finger Lakes Trail Conference
                      P.O. Box 18048
                      Rochester, NY 14618-0048
                      (716) 288-7191
                      http://www.fingerlakes.net/trailsystem

                      N.Y.S. Department of Environmental
                         Conservation – Forestry
                      7291 Coon Road
                      Bath, NY 14810-9728
                      (607) 776-2165
                      http://www.dec.state.ny.us

Birdseye Hollow County Park offers picnic tables, grills, a pavilion, playground, and outhouses. It also has a boardwalk to an observation deck in the pond, a favorite place of people fishing and birdwatchers.

The hike described is an easy ramble through the woods on a section of the Finger Lakes Trail (FLT). If you like exploring old graveyards, you're in luck. You'll pass one in the woods, with grave markers dating to the early 1800s. The return leg on the blue blazed trail can be wet in spring time and after rain storms.

137

An observation deck
extends into the pond at
Birdseye Hollow Park.

Trail Description
- From the parking area, walk back up the entrance road along the left side. You'll begin to see blue blazes.
- At a green and white "Trail" sign, the trail enters the woods, heading southeast.
- Soon continue straight as the trail turns to white blazes. (Pass a white-blazed trail to the left. This is the Finger Lakes Trail, heading north.)
- Reach Birdseye Hollow Road and turn right (S) along the road.
- Shortly after the park entrance, turn left (E) into the woods.
- The trail will parallel a creek bed.
- Follow the white blazes as they twist and turn through a young forest.
- At 0.8 mile, reach a dirt road near some mobile homes but bear left to continue in the woods.
- Quickly reach County Route 16. Turn right (W) and follow the road for a short distance, then turn left back into the woods.
- Cross an old logging road.
- Continue straight (N) past a blue trail junction. (The blue trail is a low water shortcut across a creek for people following the Finger Lakes Trail.)
- Pass an old cemetery on the right.
- At 1.4 miles, pass a cellar hole from an old farmhouse, then cross a logging road.
- Reach County Route 16 at 1.5 miles and turn left (NW) following the road.
- In about 25 yards, watch carefully for the blue trail blazes on the other side of the road (NE) and head into the woods before reaching the bridge.
- Pass an intersecting trail.
- Emerge to a grass area in the park and follow the edge of the pond back to the parking area.

Date Hiked: _____
Notes:

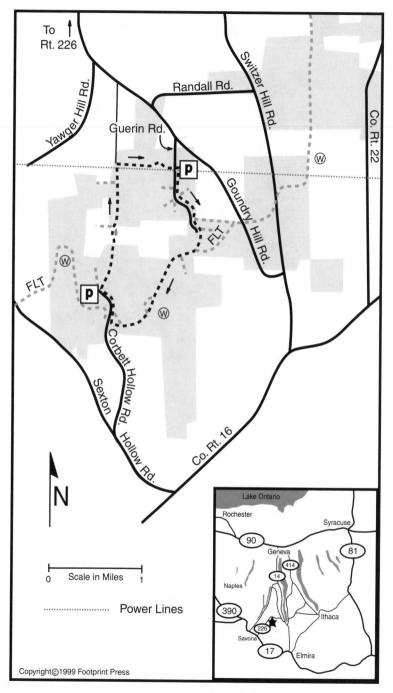

Goundry Hill State Forest

28.
Goundry Hill State Forest

Location:	Southwest of Seneca Lake, Schuyler County
Directions:	From the south end of Seneca Lake, head west on County Route 16 passing through the small towns of Townsend and Monterey. Turn north on Sexton Hollow Road. At the "Y" bear right onto Corbett Hollow Road. Park along the circle at the end of the road.

Alternative Parking: Near the power lines on Guerin Road

Hiking Time:	2.5 hours
Length:	4.5 mile loop
Difficulty:	👣 👣 👣 👣
Surface:	Dirt and grass trails
Trail Markings:	White blazes, blue and orange plastic markers
Uses:	🚶
Dogs:	OK on leash
Admission:	Free
Contact:	Finger Lakes Trail Conference P.O. Box 18048 Rochester, NY 14618-0048 (716) 288-7191 http://www.fingerlakes.net/trailsystem
	N.Y.S. Department of Environmental Conservation – Forestry 7291 Coon Road Bath, NY 14810-9728 (607) 776-2165 ext. 10 http://www.dec.state.ny.us

The 2,112 acres of Goundry Hill State Forest and the adjacent 9,085 acres of Sugar Hill State Forest are home to the Six Nations Horse and Snowmobile Trail network. The 40 miles of trails are used extensively by horses and their riders, particularly in the northern section. As a result, the majority of trails are mud wallows, ripped up by horse hoofs, and not pleasant for walking. They contain a conglomerate of trail marking methods. Trees and posts along the trail sport a wide array of blazes, markers, and signs. Each must mean something to somebody, but to a wandering walker they present a jumble of non-information.

The trail described here is in the lower, less heavily used section of Six Nation Trail. It comprises a mixture of wide logging roads, grassy paths, narrow gravel roads, and two track lanes. The definition of what constitutes a road is blurred in this area. For example, the trail follows Guerin Road for part of its path. It begins as a one lane gravel path, resembling a tree-shaded driveway more than a road. As you proceed, it becomes more dirt than gravel, then turns into parallel tracks of dirt surrounded by grass. It finally evolves into a wide grass path through the woods. At what point does it cease to be a road?

This is a refreshing woods walk, away from the bustle of modern life. The paths are mostly wide and easy walking. There are long sections of fairly level terrain interspersed with one long, steep uphill climb, and one long, steep downhill. At one point the trail detours around a flooded lowland where beavers were once active. You can see the wide path as it continues

Looking west from Guerin Road along the trail in Goundry Hill.

across the pond, once a straight shot. The markings will be a combination of rectangular, blue plastic markers and rectangular, white Finger Lakes Trail (FLT) blazes. You'll also see round, orange snowmobile markers and round, blue horse trail markers.

Part of the fun of this trail is the drive to the trailhead. Corbett Hollow Road is a narrow gravel lane that takes you deep into the hollow. Pretty homes and farms dot the way as you ride high over marshes between steep hills.

The northern section, called Sugar Hill, derived its name from the abundant sugar maple trees which once provided winter income for early settlers. Unfortunately, the shallow soils on this high land made farming unprofitable and early in the 19th century, forests began reclaiming the abandoned farmland. Conifers were planted in plantations, and are still evident today as you walk the land.

Sugar Hill has a fire tower – highest point in Schuyler County and the last remaining tower in the Finger Lakes area. You can climb it for a panoramic view of the mountains separating Keuka and Seneca Lakes. Near the tower is a network of trails and straw bales which make up an archery course.

Camping: Allowed anywhere in Goundry Hill State Forest. Obtain a free camping permit from D.E.C. in Bath for stays of three nights or more, or for groups of 10 or more individuals.

Trail Directions
- From the northwest corner of the loop at the end of Corbett Hollow Road, the trail begins as a fork. Bear right (NE) on the lower trail following rectangular blue plastic markers.
- Bear left, following the new detour trail around the pond created by beavers.
- When the detour trail meets a dirt logging road, turn right, then take a quick left (NE) to continue on your original path.
- At 0.7 mile, pass a tiny log cabin on the left.
- Continue straight (N) as the horse trail heads left.
- Pass another cabin on the left.
- At 1.2 miles, pass under power lines.
- Immediately after the power lines, turn right (E) to head uphill, parallel to the power lines. This will be a long, steep climb without the

advantage of tree cover. There are no markings along this section of trail.

- The trail will swing through the woods, then return to the power line opening as you continue uphill.
- Reach Guerin Road and turn right (S) on the single lane gravel road. Parking is available here. Round, blue horse trail markers will begin again.
- Pass a trail to the right.
- Pass a grass trail to the left, then two grass trails on the right as the road bends. The side trails are labeled with "No Trespassing" signs.
- Pass a "Private Land" sign, then another unmarked trail to the left.
- At 1.7 miles, pass a trailer, then reach a trail junction. "G Trail" heads to the left. Continue straight (S) as the road turns into "H Trail." (The D.E.C. has plans to re-label these trails so you may find this section called "Oneida Trail.")
- The road becomes two dirt tracks.
- Pass a trail on the left and continue straight (S) on what is now a grass path.
- At 2.1 miles, the white-blazed FLT comes in from the left. Bear right, staying on the wide grass Guerin Road which is now labeled with white blazes and rectangular blue plastic markers.
- At 2.4 miles, reach a "Y" and bear right (W) following the white blazes.
- Begin the long downhill.
- At 3.7 miles, reach another "Y." You can go in either direction. The branches merge in a short distance.
- Cross a small bridge over a creek, then bear left to follow the white blazes.
- At 4.1 miles reach Corbett Hollow Road. Turn right and follow the road for 0.4 mile back to the parking loop. (The white-blazed Finger Lakes Trail continues straight across Corbett Hollow Road.)

Date Hiked: _____

Notes:

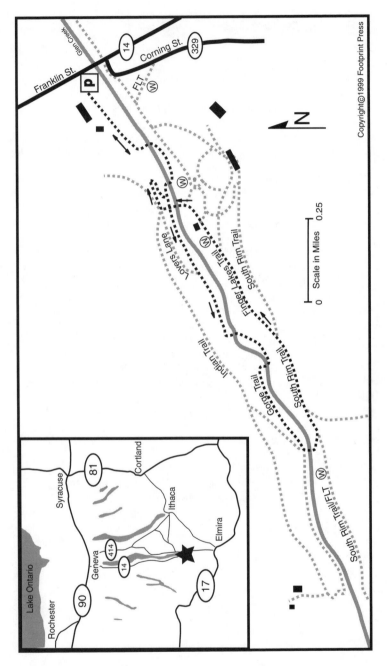

Watkins Glen State Park

29.
Watkins Glen State Park

Location: South end of Seneca Lake, Schuyler County
Directions: Route 14 becomes Franklin Street in Watkins Glen.
                  The pay parking area for Watkins Glen State Park is
                  between 9th and 10th Streets on the west side of
                  Franklin Street.
Alternative Parking: Anywhere within the town of Watkins Glen
Hiking Time: 1.5 hours
Length: 3 mile loop
Difficulty: 👣 👣 👣 👣

Surface: Stone and dirt trails
Trail Markings: Some brown and yellow signs. White blazes on the
                  Finger Lakes Trail portion.
Uses: 🚶

Dogs: Pets NOT allowed on gorge trails
Admission: Free if you park in town and walk. (Parking at the
                  trailhead costs $5 per vehicle)
Contact: Watkins Glen State Park
                  P.O. Box 304
                  Watkins Glen, NY 14891
                  (607) 535-4511

                  Finger Lakes Trail Conference
                  P.O. Box 18048
                  Rochester, NY 14618-0048
                  (716) 288-7191
                  http://www.fingerlakes.net/trailsystem

Whether it's a first time visit, or a repeat hike, you're in for a treat at this park. The strenuous trails wander through rock tunnels, behind waterfalls, over bridges above the gorge, and most importantly, alongside an incredibly spectacular gorge full of water cuts and waterfalls. There are many steps to climb, so you'll get a good aerobic workout in a short time and you may get wet from waterfall spray. The trails are closed from November 10 until mid-May when ice and snow make the journey dangerous.

145

Glen Creek tumbles through the glen.

Morvalden Ells, a journalist from Elmira, opened Watkins Glen as a private tourist resort in 1863. The rock tunnels you'll walk through were hand-cut in the early 1900s. The area became a state park in 1906. The glen began to form 12,000 years ago at the end of the ice age. Great continental glaciers from Canada excavated an immense trough in an ancient river valley, leaving behind 35-mile long Seneca Lake, the deepest of the Finger Lakes. Glen Creek has poured down the glacially steepened valley ever since, slowly eroding the weak sedimentary rock. Today Glen Creek descends 400 feet in two miles, creating 19 waterfalls and 300-foot cliffs.

The route described here follows the Gorge Trail west from the lower entrance, loops back on the Finger Lakes Trail, crosses the gorge on a suspension bridge, and continues back through the gorge to the beginning point.

Bed & Breakfasts:	Clarke House B&B, 102 Durland Place, Watkins Glen, (607) 535-7965
	The Rose Window B&B, (607) 535-4687
	Rosey Cheeks B&B, (607) 535-7809
	Seneca Lake Watch B&B, (607) 535-4490
	The Victorian B&B, (607) 535-6582
Campgrounds:	Six Nations Camping Area, Watkins Glen State Park, (800) 456-2267, http://www.park-net.com
	Warren W. Clute Memorial Park Camping Area, 521 East 4th Street, Watkins Glen, (607) 535-4438
	Watkins Glen-Corning KOA, Route 414 South, Watkins Glen, (607) 535-7404
Ice Cream:	The Pavilion, N. Franklin Street, Watkins Glen
	Great Escape Ice Cream Parlor, N. Franklin Street, Watkins Glen
	Byrne Dairy, corner Route 414 and Route 14, Watkins Glen
Outfitters:	Terrapin Outfitters, 123 3rd Street, Watkins Glen, (607) 535-5420
	Watkins Sporting Goods, 123 4th Street, Watkins Glen, (607) 535-2756

Trail Directions
- From the parking area, head up stairs through a rock tunnel.
- Cross a bridge high over the water as it digs through rock far below.

147

Notice the hole cut in the rock directly in front of the bridge. In the mid 1800s, water behind a dam passed through this flume tunnel, down a wooden trough, and over the waterwheel of a flour mill in what is now the parking area.

- Stay on the Gorge Trail, passing stairs to the left.
- Walk behind Cavern Cascade waterfall, then into a spiral tunnel.
- The suspension bridge overhead and the stairway to the right will be part of your return loop. Stay on the Gorge Trail.
- Climb though another tunnel stairway. You've entered the narrows with a unique micro-climate. It is shady, cool, and moist most of the time, almost like a rainforest.
- At 0.6 mile, pass stairs to the right that lead to Lover's Lane.
- Climb stairs and a pass through a tunnel. Then cross the bridge over Central Cascade waterfall, which plunges more than 60 feet.
- Walk under Rainbow Falls. If you're lucky enough to be here on a sunny, late afternoon, see if you can spot the rainbow.
- At 0.8 mile, cross another bridge, then walk under Pluto waterfall, named for the ancient Roman lord of the underworld. Little can grow in this dark, narrow passage.
- At 1.1 miles, cross Mile Point bridge to the Finger Lakes Trail. (The Gorge Trail continues straight for another 0.4 mile. To the right is Indian Trail.)
- Climb stairs to a "T." Turn left on the Finger Lakes Trail.
- Follow the white blazes past a trail to the right which leads to the camping area.
- Pass a shelter.
- Cross a cement bridge.
- Bear left at the "Y."
- At the next "Y' bear right, following white blazes through a picnic area.
- Pass a building and road to the right. Continue following white blazes.
- Turn left to return to the Gorge Trail at the small lily pond.
- Cross a suspension bridge 85 feet over the creek. During the great flood of 1935, the water rose to within five feet of this bridge.
- Turn right following the "main entrance" sign.
- Turn right and head down stairs.
- Turn left and continue down, following the Gorge Trail back to the parking area.

Date Hiked: _____
Notes:

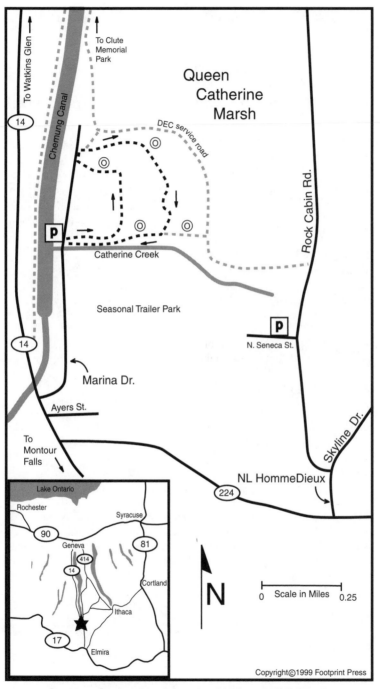

Queen Catherine Marsh - Willow Walk Trail

30.
Queen Catherine Marsh – Willow Walk Trail

Location:	Montour Falls at the south end of Seneca Lake, Schuyler County
Directions:	Take Route 14 south through Watkins Glen. At the north end of Montour Falls, turn east on Marina Drive. Pass trailers and camping areas and cross a bridge. Park on the left shortly after the bridge, facing the Chemung Canal.

Alternative Parking: A parking area on North Seneca Street

Hiking Time:	45 minutes
Length:	1.1 mile loop
Difficulty:	👣👣
Surface:	Dirt trails
Trail Markings:	Most of route is orange-blazed
Uses:	🚶 🎿
Dogs:	OK
Admission:	Free
Contact:	N.Y.S. Department of Environmental Conservation – Wildlife 7291 Coon Road Bath, NY 14810-9728 (607) 776-2165 ext. 10 http://www.dec.state.ny.us

Queen Catherine Marsh is an 882-acre protected wetland. Its man-made ditches and potholes attract shorebirds, waterfowl, muskrats, and turtles, among other wildlife. The wetlands act as a natural sponge for floodwaters, absorbing thousands of gallons of floodwater per acre. Thirty species of butterflies breed in this area.

Once called Bad Indian Swamp, this cattail swamp at the south end of Seneca Lake was saved from the ravages of developers and swamp-pavers. Its current name is a tribute to a local native tribal monarch, Queen Catherine Montour who died in 1804.

The Chemung Canal, which bisects Queen Catherine Marsh, once reached 23 miles south to Elmira. It was closed in 1887. The portion remaining today is part of the N.Y.S. Erie Canal System.

Willow Walk follows tree-shaded dikes through the wetland and passes large willow trees as it wanders through woods. This is an ideal short stroll for a hot summer day.

Campgrounds: Havana Glen Park & Campground, Route 14 South, Montour Falls, (607) 535-9476

Warren W. Clute Memorial Park Camping Area, 521 East 4th Street, Watkins Glen, (607) 535-4438

Watkins Glen-Corning KOA, Route 414 South, Watkins Glen, (607) 535-7404

Six Nations Camping Area, Watkins Glen State Park, (800) 456-2267, http://www.park-net.com

Outfitters: Terrapin Outfitters, 123 3rd Street, Watkins Glen, (607) 535-5420

Watkins Sporting Goods, 123 4th Street, Watkins Glen, (607) 535-2756

Trail Directions
- From the parking area, cross Marina Drive. Follow the sign "Observation Tower, Willow Walk X-Ski Trail" to the trail bearing left.
- Head uphill on steps. This part of the trail is orange-blazed.
- You'll be walking on a raised dike between wetlands, under a tree canopy.
- The trail bends left, away from the "Scenic Trail."
- At 0.4 mile, reach Marina Road next to the Montour Falls Yacht Club. Turn right on the road, then take a quick right following the orange blazes. Pass a "Public Hunting Grounds" sign.
- Pass a bridge on the left. Continue straight on the orange-blazed trail.
- At 1.0 mile, reach a "T" and turn right. (The orange-blazed trail goes left.)
- Reach the parking area on Marina Drive.

Date Hiked: _____
Notes:

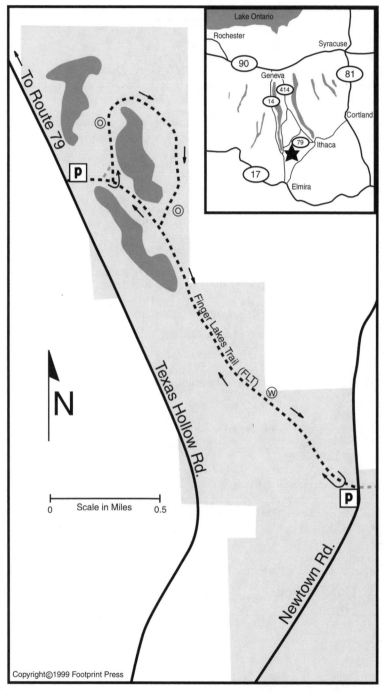

Texas Hollow State Forest

31.
Texas Hollow State Forest

Location: Southeast of Seneca Lake, Schuyler County
Directions: From Watkins Glen, follow Route 79 north. Pass through Burdett, then turn south on Texas Hollow Road. Park in front of the yellow metal barrier with a stop sign on the east side of Texas Hollow Road.
Alternative Parking: At the trail intersection on Newtown Road.
Hiking Time: 2.25 hours
Length: 4.1 mile loop
Difficulty: 👣 👣 👣 👣

Surface: Dirt trails
Trail Markings: Orange and white blazes
Uses:

Dogs: OK on leash
Admission: Free
Contact: Finger Lakes Trail Conference
P.O. Box 18048
Rochester, NY 14618-0048
(716) 288-7191
http://www.fingerlakes.net/trailsystem

N.Y.S. Department of Environmental
Conservation – Forestry
7291 Coon Road
Bath, NY 14810-9728
(607) 776-2165 ext. 10
http://www.dec.state.ny.us

This trail begins deceptively easily with a stroll around a pond and wetland, through a varied forest. It's fairly level for awhile, then the long and moderately steep climb to Newtown Road is sure to get your heart pounding. But this trail is a fine example of wilderness tranquility and pure joy to hike.

153

Texas Hollow Trail takes you to the top of the hill across the pond.

Most of the route follows the Finger Lakes Trail. Its white blazes are easy to follow. As a side loop, you'll follow square orange blazes around a pond. The orange blazes are more of a challenge to follow and the path is less well traveled. Be sure to pay attention to the blazes and look behind you or backtrack to the last blaze if you find you've lost them. At one point you'll reach a logging road with no blazes in sight. Turn right and they'll pick up again. The goal is to keep the pond to your right. It's not difficult to follow, it just requires attentiveness.

Bed & Breakfast: Towering Pines B&B, (607) 546-2656

Trail Directions
- From the yellow barrier, follow the white blazes downhill (SE) on the wide path.
- Pass the edge of a pond on the right. The hill in front of you is the one you will climb.
- Bear right (E) at the "Y" following the white blazes.
- At 0.2 mile, reach the orange-blazed trail and turn left.
- Follow the orange blazes carefully through the woods, keeping the pond to your right.
- Reach an old logging road and turn right. The orange blazes will begin again.

154

- At 0.9 mile, reach a "T" with the white-blazed trail. Turn left.
- Cross two rustic log bridges.
- The trail meanders through the woods and begins climbing steadily uphill.
- Cross several old logging roads and continue uphill after each.
- At 2.0 miles, the trail bends south to follow an old logging road for a short distance, then heads left (SE), uphill off the road.
- Reach Newtown Road at 2.3 miles. Turn around and head back downhill, following the white blazes.
- At 3.7 miles, pass the orange-blazed trail on the right.
- Pass the orange-blazed trail again at 3.9 miles.
- Pass the edge of the pond, then head uphill to the parking area at the yellow barrier.

Date Hiked: _____

Notes:

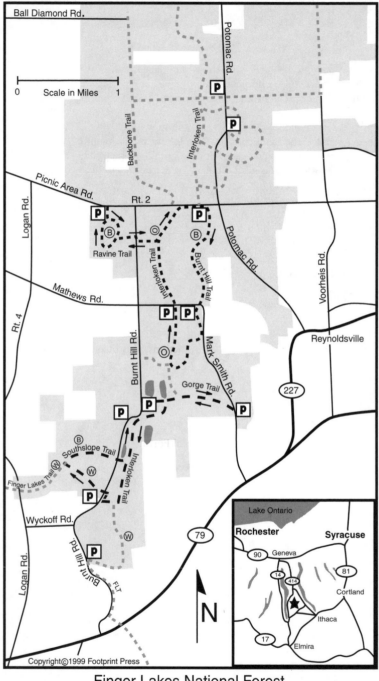

Finger Lakes National Forest
Ravine Trail Loop and Gorge Trail Loop

32.

Finger Lakes National Forest – Ravine Trail Loop

Location:	Southeast side of Seneca Lake, Schuyler County
Directions:	From Route 414, head east on County Route 2 (Picnic Area Road). The parking area for Ravine Trail is on the right, past County Route 4 (Logan Road).
Alternative Parking:	Blueberry Patch Campsite parking lot on Picnic Area Road
	Two parking lots on Matthews Road
Hiking Time:	3 hours
Length:	5.7 mile loop (combine with the Gorge Trail Loop (hike #33) for an 11.4 mile loop)
Difficulty:	👣 👣 👣
Surface:	Dirt and grass trails
Trail Markings:	Excellent signs at junctions, plus blue and orange blazes
Uses	🚶
Dogs:	OK on leash
Admission:	Free
Contact:	Finger Lakes National Forest 5218 State Route 414 Hector, NY 14841 (607) 546-4470

The Finger Lakes National Forest encompasses 16,000 acres of land and has over 30 miles of interconnecting hiking trails. Hiking during hunting season is not recommended since the national forest is open to hunting.

On foot, you can explore the deep forests and steep hills of this varied countryside. The forest contains a five-acre blueberry patch. What better treat on any excursion than devouring a handful of freshly picked blueberries? July and August are the best months to find ripe blueberries. This forest also offers overnight camping and a privately owned bed-and-breakfast nearby, making it a perfect weekend getaway. Contact the Finger Lakes National Forest for additional information on camping.

The Iroquois Indians originally inhabited the area around the Finger Lakes National Forest. In 1790 the area was divided into 600-acre military lots and distributed among Revolutionary War veterans as payment for their services. These early settlers cleared the land for production of hay and small grains such as buckwheat. As New York City grew, a strong market for these products developed, encouraging more intensive agriculture. The farmers prospered until the middle of the nineteenth century, when a series of events occurred. These included the popularity of motorized transportation in urban centers (reducing the number of horses to be fed), gradual depletion of the soil resource, and competition from midwestern agriculture due to the opening of the Erie Canal.

Between 1890 and the Great Depression, over a million acres of farmland were abandoned in south central New York State. In the 1930s it was obvious that farmers in many parts of the country could no longer make a living from their exhausted land. Environmental damage worsened as they cultivated the land more and more intensively to make ends meet. Several pieces of legislation were passed, including the Emergency Relief Act of 1933 and the Bankhead-Jones Farm Tenant Act of 1937, to address these problems. A new government agency, the Resettlement Administration, was formed to carry out the new laws. This agency not only directed the relocation of farmers to better land or other jobs, but also coordinated the purchase of marginal farmland by the federal government.

We're visitors to this beautiful valley view. The cows enjoy it year round.

158

Between 1938 and 1941, over 100 farms were purchased in the Finger Lakes National Forest area and administered by the Soil Conservation Service. Because this was done on a willing-seller, willing-buyer basis, the resulting federal ownership resembled a patchwork quilt. The land was named the Hector Land Use Area and was planted with conifers and turned into grazing fields to stabilize the soil. Individual livestock owners were allowed to graze animals on the pastureland to show how less intensive agriculture could still make productive use of the land.

By the 1950s many of the objectives of the Hector Land Use Area had been met, and the public was becoming interested in the concept of multiple uses of public land. In 1954 administration responsibilities were transferred to the U.S. Forest Service. The name was changed to the Hector Ranger District, Finger Lakes National Forest, in 1985.

Today this National Forest is used for recreation, hunting, forestry, grazing of private livestock, preservation of wildlife habitat, and education and research. It is a treasure available for us all to enjoy.

This loop starts and ends on the Ravine Trail where Tug Hollow Creek dug its way to a bed of flat slate slabs. The biggest climbs are in and out of this ravine. In between it covers flatter portions on the Interloken and Burnt Hill Trails. Most of the trail is in the woods, but a few sections take you through active cow pastures.

Across Picnic Area Road from the parking lot is the Updike Historical Site. A short walk on the trail takes you to the remains of a once prosperous farm which was owned by the Updike family for generations. It was originally built by Renselaer and Orvilla Updike in 1852 and passed to their son Alvah and his wife Harriet in 1902. The stone house foundation and concrete slab from the barn are still visible.

Bed and Breakfasts:	Red House Country Inn B&B, Picnic Area Road, (607) 546-8566
	Country Gardens B&B, (607) 535-2272
Campgrounds:	Blueberry Patch Campground within the National Forest charges a fee on a first come, first served basis. Free camping is also allowed throughout the National Forest.
	Potomac Group Campground within the National Forest, for groups up to 40 by reservation only

159

Sunset-on-Seneca Campsites, 8453 Lower Lake
Road, Lodi, (607) 582-6750

Trail Directions
- Head south on the trail following the blue blazes.
- Bear left at the "loop trail" sign.
- Cross a wooden bridge on this narrow woods trail.
- The ravine begins to form on your right.
- At 0.3 mile, turn left at the "trail" sign.
- Head down steps into the ravine. Pass a trail to the right that will become part of your return loop. Continue straight (SE) and head uphill.
- Bear left at the "trail" sign toward the top of the hill.
- Reach Burnt Hill Road at 0.7 mile.
- Turn right (S) on the road for 25 yards.
- Turn left to continue on Ravine Trail and continue a gradual uphill.
- Reach a "T" at 1.0 mile. Turn left (N) on the orange-blazed Interloken Trail.
- Bear left and stay on the orange-blazed trail. Several small side trails lead to the Blueberry Patch Campsites.
- Continue straight past a clearing and small trails on the right.
- Reach Picnic Area Road at 1.3 miles. Turn right (E) on the road.
- Pass the entrance to Blueberry Patch Campground.
- Pass the junction for Interloken Trail, continuing straight for a short distance on Picnic Area Road.
- At a parking area on the right, turn right toward Burnt Hill Trail.
- Head southeast from the parking area, then turn right (S) at the "trail" sign, walking along the edge of a pasture.
- The trail bends right, then bends left around the end of the pasture.
- At 1.9 miles follow the "trail" sign back into the woods.
- The trail bends left at the next "trail" sign.
- Continue south through a gate into South Velie pasture. This is an active cow pasture, so be sure to latch the gate behind you.
- Follow the blue blazes on posts through the pasture. Notice a pond to the left and a communication tower to the right.
- Re-enter the woods at 2.4 miles.
- Pass through a second gate, then cross Matthews Road and a parking area. Continue straight (S) through the woods.
- Cross a seasonal stream.
- The trail winds placidly through the woods, gradually downhill.
- At 3.3 miles, reach the intersection of Interloken Trail and turn right (N)

onto Interloken Trail (orange-blazed).

[Turn left here if you want to join the Ravine and Gorge Loop trails]

- Walk gradually uphill through a green tree tunnel. If it's late summer, watch for ripe berries along the way.
- At 3.8 miles, reach Matthews Road and a parking area. Cross the road.
- Cross through the pasture, following orange blazes on posts. Enjoy the panoramic view of Seneca Lake valley to your left. A big old apple tree in the pasture makes a perfect shaded break spot.

An apple tree in a pasture makes a perfect shaded break spot.

- Pass another gate and return to woods, heading downhill.
- Cross a seasonal creek bed.
- At 4.6 miles, reach Ravine Trail and turn left (W), downhill.
- Reach Burnt Hill Road. Turn right (N) for 25 yards.
- Turn left (W) to continue on the trail.
- Reach a "trail" sign at 5.2 miles. Bear right and head downhill into the gully.
- Cross a seasonal streambed.
- Turn left (SW) at the next trail junction.
- Ford the streambed of Tug Hollow Creek. If the water is low, check for fossils in the flat rocks.
- Climb out of the ravine.
- The ravine will appear on your right, far below.
- Cross a small wooden bridge.
- At 5.6 miles, pass the Ravine Loop Trail junction to the right. Continue straight.
- Reach the parking area on Picnic Area Road.

Date Hiked: _____
Notes:

33.
Finger Lakes National Forest – Gorge Trail Loop

Location:	Southeast side of Seneca Lake, Schuyler County
Directions:	From Route 414, head east on Matthews Road, then turn south on Burnt Hill Road. The parking area for Gorge Trail is on the left.
Alternative Parking:	Two other parking areas farther south on Burnt Hill Road
	The parking area on Mark Smith Road
Hiking Time:	2.7 hours
Length:	5.4 mile loop (combine with the Ravine Trail Loop (hike #32) for an 11.4 mile loop)
Difficulty:	👞 👞 👞 👞
Surface:	Dirt and grass trails
Trail Markings:	Excellent signs at junctions, plus orange, white, and blue blazes
Uses:	🚶
Dogs:	OK on leash
Admission:	Free
Contact:	Finger Lakes National Forest
	5218 State Route 414
	Hector, NY 14841
	(607) 546-4470
	Finger Lakes Trail Conference
	P.O. Box 18048
	Rochester, NY 14618-0048
	(716) 288-7191
	http://www.fingerlakes.net/trailsystem

This hike is entirely in the woods, shaded by the trees above. You start with a walk into the gorge where Hector Falls Creek carved its way to the slate bedrock. For part of the trek you'll walk a portion of the Finger Lakes Trail which stretches across New York State for 557 miles from Allegany State Park to the Catskill Mountains.

Trail Directions (see map on page 156)
- From the Gorge Trail parking area on Burnt Hill Road, head east on the trail.
- Pass a pond on your left.
- Follow the "trail" sign to the left and enter the woods.
- Pass another pond on the left. Reach a trail intersection and turn left onto Interloken Trail.
- Head downhill and cross a boardwalk.
- Cross a seasonal stream.
- At 0.3 mile, reach the second intersection of Interloken Trail. This time continue straight, uphill on Gorge Trail.
- Cross another seasonal stream.
- Head downhill.
- Cross two more seasonal streams.
- There's a steep downhill into the gorge.
- Pass two "trail" signs.
- Cross a seasonal feeder stream.
- Walk parallel with the rock-strewn streambed. (You can turn around at this point and decrease the loop length by 0.8 mile.)
- Head uphill through a pine woods.
- Walk downhill to the parking area on Mark Smith Road. You've come 1.1 miles.
- Turn around and retrace your steps, heading uphill.
- Pass the gully where water cascades down the slate slabs.
- Cross a seasonal stream and "trail" sign.
- Bear right and head uphill at the second "trail" sign.
- Cross two seasonal streams.
- Head uphill.
- Cross another seasonal stream.
- At 1.6 miles, reach the Interloken Trail junction. Continue straight on Interloken Trail.
- Cross a seasonal stream, then a boardwalk.
- At the next junction (1.7 miles), bear left on the orange-blazed Interloken Trail.
- The vegetation becomes lusher on the forest floor.
- Reach Burnt Hill Road and continue straight (W).
- Pass a pond on the left.
- Wind around the pond on a grass-covered dike.
- Re-enter the woods.
- Pass through a muddy stretch torn up by horse hooves.
- Reach the junction of Southslope Trail and continue straight (SW) on

163

Interloken Trail.
- Eventually enter a pine forest where the planted trees all form rows.
- Begin a gradual downhill as grasses line the trail.
- Reach the Finger Lakes Trail intersection at 3.0 miles. Continue straight (W) on the white-blazed FLT. (Down the trail to the left is a shelter.)
- Continue downhill.
- Reach Burnt Hill Road and turn right (NE) following the white blazes.
- The trail turns left (N) into the woods, shortly after a parking area on the left.
- Head downhill.
- Cross a seasonal feeder stream.
- Cross a wooden bridge. (You'll begin to see markers for North Country Trail. This trail will eventually extend across the country and is using portions of the Finger Lakes Trail through New York State.)
- A gradual downhill, then cross a small wooden bridge.
- At 3.7 miles, turn right (N) on Southslope Trail following the blue blazes.
- Emerge from the woods and cross through a scrub field.
- Return to the woods.
- Cross a seasonal stream, then a boardwalk.
- Cross two small culverts.
- Cross Burnt Hill Road.
- Bear right (E) at the pond.
- Cross the end of the pond on stones and continue on the blue trail.
- Follow the blue blazes through the woods and gradually uphill.
- Reach a "T" at 4.5 miles and turn left (NE) on the orange-blazed Interloken Trail.
- Pass through a muddy stretch torn up by horse hooves.
- Reach a pond and follow the grass-covered dike around it.
- Continue straight past two parking areas off Burnt Hill Road.
- Pass the Interloken Trail sign.
- At the next junction, turn left (W) on Gorge Trail. You've come 5.2 miles.
- Pass the pond on the right.
- Bear right at the "trail" sign on the grass dike around the pond.
- Reach the parking area.

Date Hiked: _____
Notes:

Walks in Wayne, Seneca, & Cayuga Counties

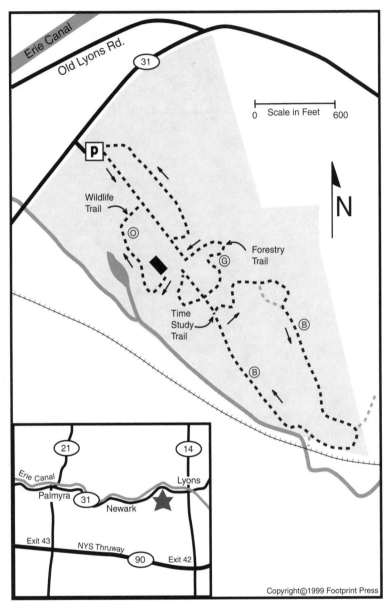

Blue Cut Nature Center

34.
Blue Cut Nature Center

Location:	Between Newark and Lyons, Wayne County
Directions:	Heading east from Newark on Route 31, Blue Cut Nature Center is on the south side of the road after Fink Road. It is marked with a large blue sign, "Blue Cut Nature Center."

Alternative Parking: None

Hiking Time:	1 hour
Length:	1.5 mile loop
Difficulty:	👢 👢 👢
Surface:	Dirt, mowed-grass, and pine needle trails
Trail Markings:	Trailheads are labeled with signs. Each trail has numbered, color-coded signs along the way.
Uses:	🚶
Dogs:	OK on leash
Admission:	Free
Contact:	Friends of Blue Cut Cornell Cooperative Extension of Wayne County 1581 Route 88 North Newark, NY 14513 (315) 331-8415

The name Blue Cut dates back to 1853 when a cut was made through a drumlin while building the railroad. The Vernon Shale had a bluish cast when exposed. Today this nature center and wildlife refuge covers over forty acres.

The 1.5-mile loop described here encompasses three trails. The blue, Time Study Trail shows that everything changes, nothing is permanent. It begins in a planted 30-year-old pine forest, then climbs a drumlin formed 11,000 years ago by glaciers. The green Forestry Trail takes you through the pine plantation. The orange Wildlife Trail shows various habitats including a wetland, woods, field, and mowed-grass strips.

167

Bed & Breakfasts: Chapman's Blue Brick Inn, 201 Scott Street, Newark, (315) 331-3226

                            Mil-Benski Farm B&B, 6769 Miller Road, Newark, (315) 331-2798

                            Peppermint Cottage B&B, 336 Pleasant Valley Road, Lyons, (315) 946-4811

                            Roselawne B&B, 101 Broad Street, Lyons, (315) 946-4218

Boat Tour: Liberty Cruises, board at Lyons Village Park for canal cruise, (315) 946-4108

Campground: Nor-Win Farm & Campsite, 2921 Pilgrimport Road, Lyons, (315) 946-4436

Trail Directions
- From the parking area, head south on the mowed-grass trail.
- Pass a grass trail on the right.
- At a "Y," bear right on the lower ground.
- Walk through a picnic area, past a pavilion. Head into the pine forest on a wide trail.
- Pass a sign for "Forestry Trail" on the right. Continue straight.
- Pass an intersection.
- Pass a blue "Time Study Trail" sign.
- Bear left at the "Y." The trail narrows and heads uphill.
- Bear left (E) at the next "Y."
- Pass a brown and yellow sign, "Danger Weapons Range." Turn right.
- Reach a "T'" and turn left (S).
- Head downhill through a shrub field.
- Reach a "T." (Left goes to a parking area.) Turn right (S).
- Re-enter the woods.
- At 0.7 mile, reach blue sign #10. (A trail to the left goes to a creek and active railroad tracks.) Continue straight.
- Bear left at the "Y."
- Re-enter the pine forest.
- Pass a trail intersection.
- Turn left under the green "Forestry Trail" sign.
- Cross the wide pine forest trail.
- The trail loops back to the picnic area, passing restrooms.
- Pass the pavilion heading west toward an orange and white arrow sign.
- Turn right just before the pond. (In the pond, check for nesting geese

and beaver activity.)
- At 1.4 miles, reach the main mowed-grass trail and turn right.
- At the "Y," bear left on the higher ground.
- Quickly turn left (E) on the mowed grass trail.
- Follow it back to the parking area.

Date Hiked: _____

Notes:

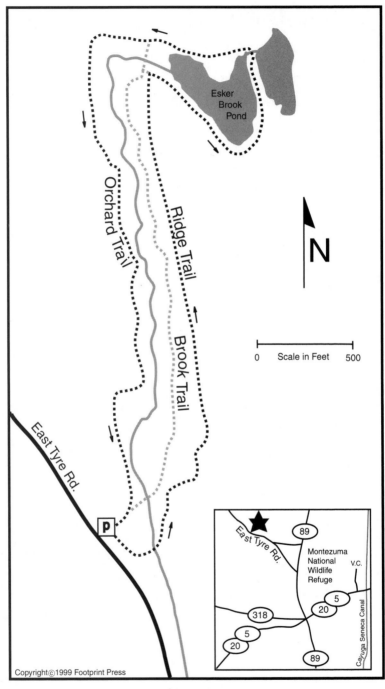

Esker Brook Nature Trail

35.
Esker Brook Nature Trail

Location:	Montezuma National Wildlife Refuge, at the north end of Cayuga Lake, (5 miles east of Seneca Falls), Seneca County
Directions:	From Route 5 & 20, turn north on Route 89, then turn west on East Tyre Road. A gravel parking area is on the right side of East Tyre Road, near a large brown and white sign, "Esker Brook Nature Trail, Montezuma National Wildlife Refuge."

Alternative Parking: None
Hiking Time: 30 minutes
Length: 1.5 mile loop
Difficulty: 👣 👣
                👣 👣

Surface: Dirt
Trail Markings: Signs at intersections
Uses: 🚶

Dogs: OK on leash
Admission: Free
Contact: Refuge Manager
                Montezuma National Wildlife Refuge
                395 Routes 5 and 20 East
                Seneca Falls, NY 13148
                (315) 568-5987
                http://www.fws.gov/r5mnwr

Montezuma National Wildlife Refuge serves as a major resting and breeding area for water birds as they migrate in the spring and fall. It is situated in one of the most active flight lanes in the Atlantic Flyway. The glaciers that scoured this area some 10,000 years ago dug the Finger Lakes and left shallow, marshy areas at the ends of the lakes. Construction of a dam at the northern end of Cayuga Lake and building of the New York State Barge Canal caused major changes to the once extensive marshes of Montezuma. By the early 1900s, all but a small portion had been drained. In 1937 the

171

Bureau of Biological Survey, which later became the U.S. Fish and Wildlife Service, bought 6,432 acres of the former marsh. The Civilian Conservation Corps began work on a series of low dikes to hold water and restore parts of the marsh.

Today, water levels are carefully manipulated in the refuge's 3,500 acres of diked pools, to ensure that migrating birds will find suitable food and nesting habitat. In 1976 Montezuma began participating in a bald eagle release program. Over four years, 23 eagles were released and have since used Montezuma to successfully rear their young.

So why is a marsh in upstate New York called Montezuma? In the early 1800s Dr. Peter Clark, a physician from New York City, came to the area because of the salt deposits recently discovered under the marshes. He built a 12-room home (a mansion for the times) on a drumlin with a view of the marshes. Dr. Clark had traveled extensively and named his estate Montezuma in honor of the last Aztec emperor and the large marshes that surrounded Mexico City.

While at Montezuma National Wildlife Refuge for your hike, be sure to check out the other attractions. A visitor center is located off Routes 5 and 20, west of the Cayuga Seneca Canal. It is packed with exhibits and well

At the northern end the trail encircles Esker Brook Pond.

worth a stop. From a spotting scope on the roof, you're likely to see nesting eagles or osprey. This is also the start of the 3.5 mile wildlife drive. A brochure available at the visitor center details the sights along the way.

Spring migration of waterfowl occurs from late February through April when 85,000 Canada geese, 12,000 snow geese, and many species of ducks use Montezuma as their southbound resting spot. Best viewing times are early morning and late afternoon. Warblers migrate in mid-May and can best be viewed from Esker Brook Nature Trail from dawn until mid-morning. April through June is wildflower season. Watch for violets, trilliums, mayapples, vetches, and mustards along the trail.

Summer is the time for waterfowl nesting. Broods of Canada geese and ducks begin to appear in early May. Great blue herons nest in the flooded timber area of Tschache Pool. Late July is peak season for the blooms of purple loosestrife, iris, mallow, and white water lily.

Fall begins the southern migration. From mid-September until freeze-up, 50,000 Canada geese and 150,000 ducks pass through the area. For shorebirds and wading birds, peak migration is mid-September. Again, they're best viewed in early morning or late afternoon.

The trails around Esker Brook are easy-to-follow dirt trails that are open for hiking only, from January through October. They're well maintained and well marked with signs. This is a wetland area so you may be wise to wear bug repellent. The esker you'll walk was formed when a river flowed under the glacier in an icy tunnel. Rocky material accumulated on the tunnel beds, and when the glacier melted, a ridge of rubble remained. All three trails lead through abandoned apple orchards to two man-made ponds.

In summer you'll see purple loosestrife along edges of the wetland, including Esker Brook Pond. This is a non-native pest plant which is aggressive. It has been spreading through northern New York State rapidly. Although pretty to look at, it pushes out native plants.

Bed and Breakfasts: The Guion House B&B, 32 Cayuga Street, Seneca Falls, (800) 631-8919

Van Cleef Homestead B&B, 86 Cayuga Street, Seneca Falls, (800) 323-8668

Ileen's B&B, 69 Cayuga Street, Seneca Falls, (315) 568-6092

Hubbell House B&B, 42 Cayuga Street, Seneca Falls, (315) 568-9690

Campgrounds: Oak Orchard Marina & Campground, Route 89 North, Seneca Falls, (315) 365-3000

Cayuga Lake State Park, 2662 Lower Lake Road, Seneca Falls, (315) 568-5163

Cayuga Lake Campgrounds, Route 89, Seneca Falls, (315) 568-2569

Trail Directions
- Head south into the woods from the parking area on the Ridge Trail. There will be a brown and yellow sign on a post saying "Ridge Trail."
- Cross a wooden bridge over Esker Brook.
- You'll pass many interpretive signs along the way.
- Head slightly uphill along a rail fence on a 12-foot wide mowed path.
- Pass a rustic wooden bench on the right.
- Reach a "T." Turn right (E) toward the pond.
- Follow the mowed area close to the pond.
- Bear left around the end of the pond, then walk between two ponds.
- Cross a wooden bridge.
- Re-enter the woods.
- A trail to the left goes to a small observation platform.
- Reach a junction. (Left goes to Brook Trail, which returns to the parking lot on the east side of Esker Brook.) Continue straight on Orchard Trail.
- Reach a bench on the right. Esker Brook will be on your left.
- Pass several interpretive signs.
- At the junction with Brook Trail, bear right to return to the parking area.

Date Hiked: _____

Notes:

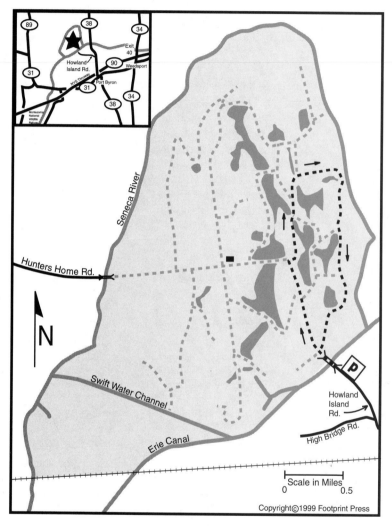

Howland Island

36.
Howland Island

Location: Three miles northwest of Port Byron, Cayuga County
Directions: From Port Byron (between exits 40 & 41 on the
                     N.Y.S. Thruway), head north on Route 38. Turn west
                     on Howland Island Road and follow it to the closed
                     bridge. Park along the right side of the road before the
                     bridge.
Alternative Parking: At the west entrance on Hunters Home Road (an
                     extension of Carn Cross Road).
Hiking Time: 2 hours
Length: 3.9 mile loop
Difficulty: 👢 👢 👢

Surface: Dirt, gravel, and grass trails
Trail Markings: None
Uses:

Dogs: OK
Admission: Free
Contact: Howland Island Wildlife Area
                     N.Y.S. Department Of Environmental Conservation
                     1285 Fisher Avenue
                     Cortland, NY 13045
                     (607) 753-3095
                     http://www.dec.state.ny.us

Waters of the Seneca River and the Erie (Barge) Canal surround the 3,100 acres of Howland Island. The land was first settled and cleared for farming in the 1800s. Farming continued until the 1920s. The land was purchased as a game refuge in 1932 and became a Civilian Conservation Corps (C.C.C.) camp between 1933 and 1941. The C.C.C. built 18 earthen dikes to create about 300 acres of water impoundments.

The rolling hills and steep drumlins above these impoundments are now home to a second growth mixture of hardwoods such as maple, ash, willow, basswood, black locust, oak, and hickory. The trails are abandoned gravel

176

This old bridge over the Erie Canal is closed to cars but remains
a perfect access to Howland Island for bicyclers and hikers.

roads and old service vehicle tracks, now sufficiently overgrown to make
pleasant hiking trails.

Through the 1930s and 1940s, Howland Island was home to an extensive pheasant farm operation that produced both eggs and pheasants. In
1951 a special waterfowl research project was begun to propagate duck
species exotic to New York. Since 1962 the area has been managed for the
natural production of waterfowl.

Hunting is allowed on portions of Howland Island so be sure to wear colorful clothing if you venture out during May or from mid-October through
November. If you encounter signs saying "Baited Area, hunting or entry
within posted area prohibited," you can ignore them. D.E.C. personnel
clarified that hunting is prohibited in these areas, but walking and bicycling
are allowed.

Campground: Hejamada Family RV Park, RD 1 McDonald Road,
                Port Byron, (315) 776-5887

Trail Directions
• From Howland Island Road, walk across the bridge over the Erie Canal.
• Pass a grass trail to the right. (This will be part of your return loop.)

177

- At 0.7 mile, pass a trail to the right, then a grass trail to the left. Continue straight on the gravel road.
- Pass a yellow metal gate at 0.9 mile.
- Reach a "T" and turn right. The trail bed will change to two gravel tracks in grass.
- Walk between ponds.
- Bear right at a "Y" and head downhill.
- Cross between two more ponds and reach another "Y." Bear right, uphill on the grass trail.
- You'll enter a pleasant green tunnel and a long gradual downhill.
- Pass a pond.
- At 2.6 miles, reach a "Y" and bear left past a pond.
- Continue straight past a trail junction.
- Pass another pond.
- Pass a yellow metal gate.
- Reach the gravel road and turn left to cross the bridge back to the parking area.

A green tunnel on Howland Island.

Date Hiked: _____

Notes:

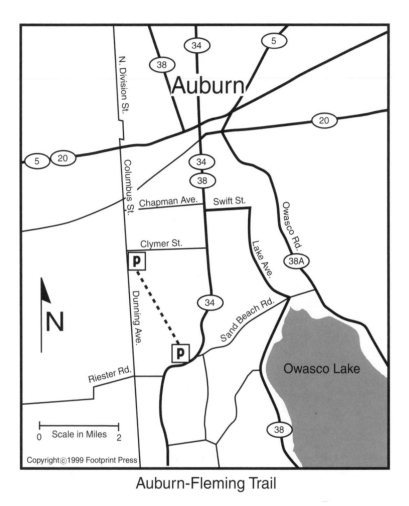

Auburn-Fleming Trail

37.
Auburn – Fleming Trail

Location: South of Auburn, Cayuga County
Directions: From Routes 5 & 20, turn south on Columbus Street.
                   Parking is on the east side of Dunning Avenue, south
                   of Clymer Street. It is marked by a brown sign with
                   yellow lettering, "Cayuga County Trail, Auburn –
                   Fleming."
Alternative Parking: Route 34, southwest of Sand Beach Road
Hiking Time: 60 minutes
Length: 2 miles round trip
Difficulty:

Surface: Dirt and cinder trail
Trail Markings: None
Uses:

Dogs: OK
Admission: Free
Contact: Tom Higgins, County Planner
                   Cayuga County Planning Board
                   160 Genesee Street
                   Auburn, NY 13021-1276
                   (315) 253-1276

                   Michele Beilman
                   Cayuga County Parks and Trails Commission
                   East Lake Road
                   Auburn, N.Y. 13021
                   (315) 253-5611

The Auburn – Fleming Trail uses an abandoned railroad bed. There's not much elevation change, but the terrain rolls and is populated with enough deteriorating railroad ties to make the walk interesting. It's a pleasant walk in a four-foot wide tunnel through trees.

Bed and Breakfasts: Springside Inn, Route 38 South, Auburn,
(315) 252-7247

Irish Rose, Auburn, (315) 255-0196

Angel's Rest B&B, Auburn, (315) 255-9188

Trail Directions

- The trail begins behind (W) the sign, with a walk over old wooden ties buried in the ground.
- After 0.25 mile, cross a stream on a metal grate bridge.
- A marsh will be on the left. Cross its outlet over a wooden railroad tie bridge.
- Cross a second railroad tie bridge.
- Unmarked trails lead off to the left. (Please stay on the Auburn – Fleming Trail. The trails to the left are on private property.) Continue straight.
- There's a dip in the trail, then a farm lane crossing.
- Cross another bridge of railroad ties over a creek.
- The trail begins to roll up and down like a roller coaster.
- A trail to the right heads to a farm.
- Pass some small side loops carved by mountain bikers.
- The trail ends at Route 34. Turn around and retrace your path.

Date Hiked: _____

Notes:

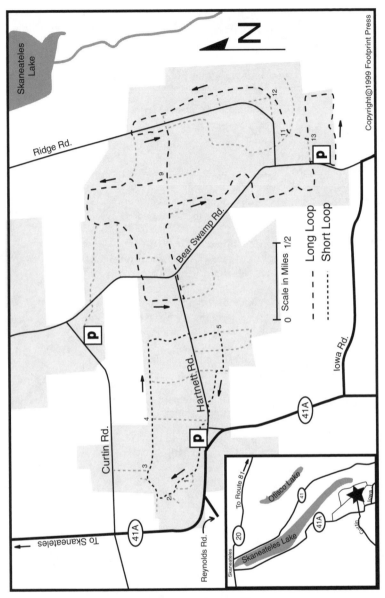

Skaneateles Lake

N

Ridge Rd.

Bear Swamp Rd.

12

11

13

P

9

0   Scale in Miles   1/2

– – – Long Loop
·········· Short Loop

Iowa Rd.

5

Hartnett Rd.

P

Curtin Rd.

4

41A

3

P

2

1

To Skaneateles

41A

Reynolds Rd.

To Route 81

20

Otisco Lake

41

41A

Skaneateles

Skaneateles Lake

Iowa

Curtin

Bear Swamp State Forest
Short Loop and Long Loop

38.
Bear Swamp State Forest – Short Loop

Location:	At the southwest end of Skaneateles Lake, Cayuga County
Directions:	From Skaneateles, head south on Route 41A. Pass Curtin Road and Reynolds Road. Turn left on the next unmarked dirt road. A brown and yellow D.E.C. sign is on the right side of Route 41A, "Bear Swamp State Forest." Park along the dirt road where you see a wooden kiosk at the trailhead on the left side of the road.

Alternative Parking: Anywhere along the dirt road (Hartnett Road)

Hiking Time:	2 hours
Length:	3.4 mile loop
Difficulty:	👣 👣 👣
Surface:	Dirt trails
Trail Markings:	Two-inch round yellow disks with black lettering, "N.Y.S. Environmental Conservation Ski Trail." Also, many intersections have six-inch brown signs with yellow numbers posted on trees above head level.
Uses:	🚶 🚴 ⛷ 🏇
Dogs:	OK
Admission:	Free
Contact:	N.Y.S. Department of Environmental Conservation P.O. Box 5170, Fisher Road Cortland, NY 13045-5170 (607) 753-3095 http://www.dec.state.ny.us

This 3,316-acre state forest is traversed by 13 miles of trails through shady forest. Over 10,000 years ago the glaciers sculpted the Finger Lakes, leaving steep valley walls and flat-topped ridges. Native Americans used this area as hunting grounds. After the Revolutionary War, veterans and their families cleared the forests and settled the area. Farming continued through

183

the Civil War and slowly declined as the soil was depleted, until the Great Depression of 1929 hastened farm abandonment. As with other State Forest land, this land was purchased in the 1930s and replanted by the Civilian Conservation Corps with red pine, Norway spruce, and larch. You'll pass through these replanted forests, now a mix of conifers and hardwoods.

Bear Swamp State Forest is managed using the multiple-use concept. This includes maintaining wildlife habitat, harvesting wood products, and encouraging recreational uses. The roads in Bear Swamp State Forest are rough but navigable by a vehicle. They are seasonal-use roads that are not plowed in the winter.

The trails are well marked with round, yellow ski trail markers. When in doubt, follow the marked trail. Hills tend to be long but not particularly steep. It can be muddy after rain.

Trail Directions (short, dark dashed lines)
• Head north on the trail past the wooden kiosk.
• Cross a wooden bridge.
• Cross a corduroy bridge.
• Cross two more wooden bridges.
• After 0.4 mile, reach intersection #1. (Numbered signs are on trees above head level.)
• Turn right to stay on the marked trail, which is an old logging road. Notice the stumps and cut treetops where wood was harvested for firewood and pulpwood.
• At 0.6 mile, reach a junction and turn right to stay on the marked trail.
• Shortly reach intersection #2 and bear right on the marked trail, an old fire road. This road is a relic of the 1930s when the young conifer plantation needed fire lanes for access and protection.
• Reach a "T" intersection at 0.8 mile and turn right.
• Around 1 mile, watch carefully. Follow the markers going right, leaving the well-trodden trail.
• Reach intersection #3 and turn right (S) on the wider trail. Notice the thinned, hardwood forest to the west as compared to the crowded, unmanaged red pine forest to the east.
• Shortly the trail bends left (E) and heads downhill.
• At 1.5 miles, a trail will head off to the right. Continue straight (SE), downhill.

184

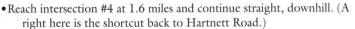
- Reach intersection #4 at 1.6 miles and continue straight, downhill. (A right here is the shortcut back to Hartnett Road.)
- Continue straight past a trail off to the right.
- Cross several bog areas with makeshift bridges.
- At 2.4 miles, cross a flowing spring. Head uphill.
- Reach Hartnett Road (a small gravel road) and turn right, uphill. Immediately, look for a trail to the left and follow it uphill through a young hardwood forest of native maple, ash, and cherry trees.
- Reach intersection #5 at 2.8 miles and turn right, uphill.
- Cross a gravel road and continue straight, uphill.
- At 3.0 miles, reach a "T" and turn right (N).
- Shortly the marked trail veers left. (Straight goes to a road.)
- At 3.2 miles, reach Hartnett Road but turn left and continue on the trail, parallel to the road.
- Emerge onto the road and bear left on Hartnett Road.
- Pass a trail to the right, then arrive at the parking area.

Date Hiked: _____

Notes:

39.
Bear Swamp State Forest – Long Loop

Location:	At the southwest end of Skaneateles Lake, Cayuga County
Directions:	From Route 41A head south past Curtin Road, Reynolds Road, and the Colonial Lodge. Turn left on Iowa Road. Take the first left on Bear Swamp Road. The parking area will be on the right up 0.2 mile.
Alternative Parking:	At any road/trail intersection, or the parking area on Curtin Road.
Hiking Time:	4 hours
Length:	7.8 mile loop
Difficulty:	🥾 🥾 🥾 🥾
Surface:	Dirt trails
Trail Markings:	Two-inch round yellow disks with black lettering, "N.Y.S. Environmental Conservation Ski Trail." Also, many intersections have six-inch brown signs with yellow numbers posted on trees above head level.
Uses:	🚶 🚴 🎿 🐎
Dogs:	OK
Admission:	Free
Contact:	N.Y.S. Department of Environmental Conservation P.O. Box 5170, Fisher Road Cortland, NY 13045-5170 (607) 753-3095 http://www.dec.state.ny.us

Trail Directions (long, dark dashed lines on the page 182 map)
- From the south parking lot on Bear Swamp Road, head southwest past a yellow sign, "motorized vehicles prohibited." Bear Swamp Road will be on your right.
- The trail bends left and heads uphill.
- Cross a small wooden bridge and continue uphill.
- Pass through a forest of red pine and Norway spruce planted in 1932–

186

1933. Notice the old stone walls to your right (NE) in the dense woods.

- The trail, an old fire lane, bends left (N) and heads gradually downhill.
- The trail bends left (W) and heads uphill.
- Crest the hill and head down. Notice the large fern field to the right.
- At the next junction (#13), turn right (N), uphill. (Left returns to the parking area.) You've completed 1 mile.
- Reach intersection #11 and continue straight (NE). Follow the markers uphill to a crest and then down.
- The trail bends left and heads uphill again.
- At 1.4 miles, reach intersection #12. Turn right (E) and follow the markers downhill.
- The trail bends left, dips, then begins a long, slow climb.
- Continue straight, past a trail to the left, for a long, slow down.
- Continue uphill past a trail to the left. The trail narrows and begins to roll.
- At 2.4 miles, cross a bridge. When the leaves are off the trees, there's a view of Skaneateles Lake from this area.
- At 2.5 miles, turn left, following the markers. The trail continues straight here so watch carefully.
- After a steep uphill, cross Ridge Road. Bear left on the marked trail that runs parallel to Ridge Road heading south.
- Head through a pine woods.
- At 2.9 miles, reach a "T" and turn right (W) on a wide dirt trail.
- After a speed bump, reach intersection #9. Turn right and cross another speed bump.
- At 3.5 miles, pass an old stone foundation. Notice the myrtle and old apple trees. They remind us that this once was the site of a farm house.
- Reach a "T" and turn left. This section is not as hilly but can be dotted with huge mud puddles during wet times of the year.
- At 4.1 miles, reach a trail junction and bear left. (Right goes to Curtin Road and a parking area.)
- Stay on the wide dirt trail as a trail heads off on the right.
- A long downhill will turn into a grass path.
- Cross Bear Swamp Road at 4.9 miles, then another long downhill.
- Cross a wooden bridge.
- At 5.3 miles, cross Hartnett Road. Immediately across the road turn left (E) and parallel Hartnett Road.
  [**Side Trip:** The trail straight is a four minute walk to a picturesque overlook of the Bear Mountain Swamp with its balsam fir, swamp-

187

meadow grass, and alder patches.]
- The trail will be level, followed by a short, steep downhill.
- Cross a small dirt road and continue straight.
- Cross a wooden bridge before crossing Bear Swamp Road at 5.5 miles.
- You're heading northeast up a long hill.
- Continue straight past the next trail intersection on the right.
- Cross a streambed.
- Traverse rolling terrain on a narrow woods path.
- Several logging trails intersect. Stay on the marked trail.
- At 6.5 miles, turn left (S) on a wide trail.
- At 6.8 miles, stay on the marked trail as it turns right, off the wide trail.
- At 6.9 miles, cross Bear Swamp Road and continue straight, downhill through fields of jewelweed on the forest floor.
- At 7.7 miles, cross Bear Swamp Road again. Take an immediate right on the trail parallel to Bear Swamp Road, heading south, back to the parking area.

Date Hiked: _____

Notes:

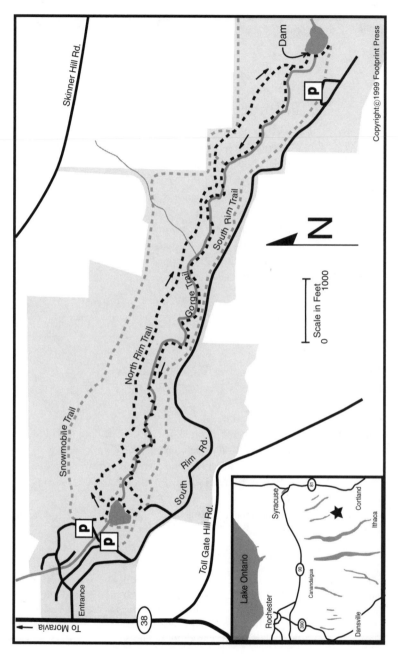

Fillmore Glen State Park

40.
Fillmore Glen State Park

Location: South of Moravia (the south end of Owasco Lake), Cayuga County

Directions: From Route 38, turn east into Fillmore Glen State Park. After the entrance gate, bear right. Take the first left at a sign for "old bath house." Pass through the first parking area, cross through (yes, through) the stream, and park in the back parking area.

Alternative Parking: At the turn-around loop at the end of South Rim Road, near the dam.

Hiking Time: 2 hours

Length: 3.7 mile loop

Difficulty: 👣 👣 👣 👣

Surface: Dirt trail

Trail Markings: Wooden signs at some intersections

Uses: 🚶

Dogs: OK on leash

Admission: $5 entry fee is charged from 9:00 AM until 6:00 PM, 7 days a week. The fee is charged only on weekends before Memorial Day and after Labor Day. No fee is charged from late October until the second week in May.

Contact: Fillmore Glen State Park
RD #3, P.O. Box 26
Moravia, NY 13118
(315) 497-0130

Ten thousand years ago as glaciers retreated from the area, their melt waters poured off Summer Hill down steep slopes to the Owasco inlet valley. The torrents cut their way through soft shale, sandstone, and even limestone in their rush to the valley below. The result is the spectacular geologic formation we know today as Fillmore Glen.

190

Water tumbles through Fillmore Glen.

The abundant plant life of the gorge caught the attention of physician Dr. Charles Atwood, an amateur botanist. He worked to establish a park in the 1920s. The trails were opened in 1921. In 1925 the 39-acre site was transferred to state ownership.

Today Fillmore Glen State Park covers 938 acres and is managed by the Office of Parks, Recreation, and Historic Preservation. The three trails, each 1.8-miles long, begin in the valley and rise 349 feet to a man-made dam at an elevation of 1,720 feet. The Gorge Trail follows the water's path. The North and South Rim Trails each follow their respective rims. The creek, which flows through the gorge and did the sculpting you're about to see, was given the unlikely name of Dry Creek.

Dry Creek is dammed twice. The first dam at the upper (E) end is to control water flow. The second dam at the lower (W) end creates a swimming hole. Be sure to bring your bathing suit for a dip after a hot climb. Behind the swimming area is the Cowsheds, a cavern of carved rock formed by the rushing waters and a high cascading waterfall. Legend has it that cows from neighboring farms took refuge in the coolness of the rock cavern during hot summer days, hence the name Cowsheds. It's well worth the short walk to see this unique area.

This park is named after our thirteenth president, Millard Fillmore. He was born in 1800 in a log cabin about five miles from the park. You'll pass a replica of his cabin on your way into the parking area.

Campground: Fillmore Glen State Park, 1-800-456-2267

Ice cream: Dee-Dee's Ice Cream, Route 38 North, Moravia, (315) 497-3543

Trail Directions
- Follow the gravel path (S) from the parking area toward the old stone bathhouse.
- Pass the bathhouse (with restrooms) and head uphill. (Swimming area is on the right.)
- At the sign "North Rim Trail," turn right and head up the slate stairs.
- The trail switchbacks through the woods as you climb out of the gorge. Breathe in deeply the aroma of pine. At this point, who has a choice? You're guaranteed to be breathing heavily anyway.
- Reach another section of steps.
- Reach the top of the gorge and the trail levels out as you proceed through a hemlock and maple forest. The steep sides of the gorge will be on your right.
- Watch for a brown and yellow sign, "North Rim Trail," and bear left, uphill.
- Cross a small wooden bridge. Then the terrain becomes hilly.
- A feeder stream will appear on the right, cutting through the bedrock. Cross on a large wooden bridge.
- Wind back to the edge of the gorge.
- Cross a small wooden bridge.
- Cross a small stream on slate steps.
- Reach a "Y" and bear left, continuing on the rim. (Right switchbacks down to the Gorge Trail – a shortcut back.)
- Cross three small wooden bridges.
- Keep right as two snowmobile trails enter from the left.
- Cross a small stream on stones.
- Bear right at a "trail" sign and head downhill.
- At a "T," turn left to head to the dam. Continue downhill.
- At a trail junction, bear left, downstairs, to cross a large wooden bridge. (The trail to the right gives a view of a waterfall.)

- Head up two flights of stairs.
- The trail crosses over the cement dam with two waterfalls on the backside. You've come 1.8 miles.
- Past the dam, head up stairs to a shelter. (The trail past the shelter goes uphill to South Rim Road and an alternate parking spot.)

Crossing the dam above Fillmore Glen.

- Turn around and head back over the dam and down to the sign directing "North Rim Trail right and Gorge Trail left." Bear left on Gorge Trail.
- Head downhill. Turn right at the "T" so the water is to your left. (The trail to the left follows the gorge to a washout area.)
- Head down stairs.
- Cross a small bridge and climb some stairs.
- Cross another small bridge and then head down stairs. Notice that the forest floor is covered with jewelweed and horsetail.
- Cross two small wooden bridges.
- The North Rim Trail cutover is on the right. Stay left.
- A bridge to the left heads to a shelter and the South Rim Trail. Continue straight, down stairs.
- Notice the moss-covered shale cliffs towering across the creek and how the water spreads flat on the bedrock platforms and cascades over the drop-offs. The Civilian Conservation Corps built the walkway you're on in the 1930s. Be sure to stop and look behind you.
- Take a natural shower as water trickles over the shale ledge along the right of the trail.
- At the base of the next set of stairs, stop to enjoy the beauty of the waterfalls.
- Head up steps to a level area.
- Head down steps and cross a bridge to the other side of the glen. You'll cross the glen a total of eight times before reaching the bottom.

Trenton and Travis Reed play in the natural shower along the glen walls.

- Head down steps to a section of trail in the streambed, behind a retaining wall.

193

- To the right is an observation area overlooking the Cowsheds area.
- Head up steps and emerge at a pavilion and restroom area.
- Before the pavilion, turn right and head down a long flight of stairs.
- Cross a bridge above the swimming area.
- Turn left after the bridge.

  [To the right is a two minute side trip to the Cowsheds.]
- Pass the swimming area on your left, the North Rim Trail to your right, and the old bathhouse to your right as you follow the path back to the parking area.

Date Hiked: _____

Notes:

Walks in Onondaga County

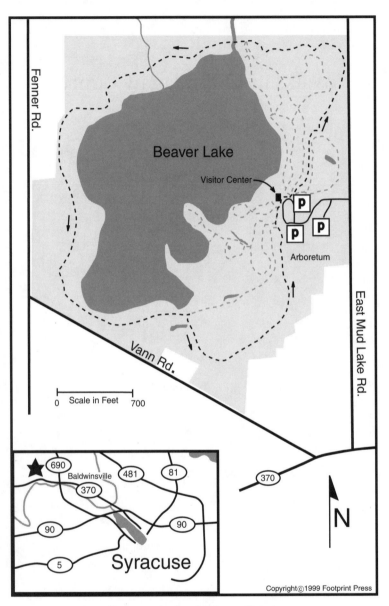

Beaver Lake Nature Center

41.
Beaver Lake Nature Center

Location:	West of Baldwinsville, (20 miles northwest of Syracuse), Onondaga County
Directions:	From Route 370 (west off Route 690), turn north on Mud Lake Road. The Nature Center entrance is on the west side of East Mud Lake Road.
Alternative Parking:	None
Hiking Time:	90 minutes
Length:	3.3 mile loop
Difficulty:	🥾 🥾
Surface:	Bark mulch trails and boardwalks
Trail Markings:	Black and white signs on posts
Uses:	🚶 🎿 ♿
Dogs:	Pets NOT allowed
Admission:	$1 per vehicle entrance fee
Contact:	Beaver Lake Nature Center 8477 East Mud Lake Road Baldwinsville, NY 13027 (315) 638-2519 http://www.co.onondaga.ny.us

Beaver Lake Nature Center is a 650-acre natural community of pond, swamp, and woodland. The glacially formed lake offers a haven for thousands of migrating Canada geese in the spring and fall. Wood ducks and barred owls nest in the surrounding hardwood forest.

There are eight loop trails available to hike. The path described below follows the outer loop and takes in parts of three trails: Deep Woods Trail, Lake Loop Trail, and Three Meadows Trail. Or choose your own route, shortening or lengthening your stay to suit your energy level and time available. All the trails are easy-to-follow and well marked, so wander with peace of mind and savor the natural surroundings.

Lakeview Trail is a 0.3 mile figure eight that leads to the shore of Beaver Lake. This trail is wheelchair accessible and is lined with interpretive signs which provide an introduction to this forest and lake community. On the shore is an observation platform with a telescope for wildlife observation.

Hemlock Hollow Trail is a 0.4 mile loop through a cool, shaded hemlock forest. A side trip from Hemlock Hollow is the 0.6-mile Bog Trail. Traverse this soggy floor on a boardwalk to an observation tower with a telescope. Along the way you can marvel at the pitcher plants and lady slipper orchids which are unique to bog environments. Refer to Moss Lake (pages 61-62) for more information on bogs.

Enjoy a sunny stroll on the 1.5 mile loop of Three Meadows Trail. You'll descend into a quarried basin, a seasonal wetland reclaimed by shrubby growth and populated by a variety of songbirds.

A pine forest, cedar/hemlock swamp, and a northern hardwood forest are the three different woodland communities you'll find along the 1.1 mile Woodland Trail. Or follow the Deep Woods Loop for 1.4 miles through the serenity of a maturing forest. A boardwalk takes you safely through a wet area with sensitive and cinnamon fern. Visit the observation blind on the shore of Beaver Lake.

Dick and Ginny Freeman complete their hike
in Beaver Lake Nature Center.

See the lake from every angle along the 3.0 mile Lake Loop. Over 0.75 mile of boardwalk lets you march through a wetland without getting your feet wet.

With a diverse aquatic environment, the Beaver Lake Nature Center is home to seven species of frogs. The tiny spring peepers are only one inch long but make themselves known with deafening "peeps" as they breed in April. These tree frogs have disks on their toes for climbing trees and a readily recognizable dark "X" mark on their backs. Gray tree frogs are twice the size of spring peepers. They reside in tall trees and sing with a birdlike trill for two seconds. Leopard frogs like the grassy areas of the nature center. You'll find wood frogs on the forest floor with long legs and a dark, raccoon-like mask over their eyes. Wood frogs come out at night to hunt insects and worms, then retreat beneath the leaf litter of the forest floor to escape the heat of day. In the water you'll find green frogs and bullfrogs. Green frogs grow to four inches long and sound like plucked banjo strings. Bullfrogs grow twice as large and bellow a deep "Jug-o-rum, Jug-o-rum."

Beaver Lake Nature Center also has seven species of snakes, none of them poisonous. Among them are garter snakes, ribbon snakes, northern water snakes, and milk snakes. Chances are if you see a snake, it will be a garter snake. Their name derives from the stripes along their bodies which resemble the fancy garters gentlemen used to wear to support their socks. Ribbon snakes resemble the garters but are more slender and seldom wander far from water. The northern water snake is dark-colored, thick bodied, and can grow up to 30 inches long. Brightly colored milk snakes are less common, but are distinctive with their red or copper blotches on a tan or gray background. The name derives from dairy farmers who blamed the snake for low milk production. Rather than steal milk, this snake was in the barns hunting rodents. Their stomachs can only hold a few tablespoons of liquid.

The Beaver Lake Nature Center is open year round (except Christmas Day) from 7:30 AM to dusk. In addition to nine miles of well-tended and marked hiking trails, the center offers summer canoeing, guided outings with naturalists, and exhibits.

Bed and Breakfast: Pandora's Getaway, 83 Oswego Street, Baldwinsville, (888) 638-8668

Boat Tours: Mid-Lakes Navigation Co., 11 Jordan Street, Skaneateles, (800) 545-4318

Canoe tours available at Beaver Lake Nature Center

Campgrounds: Sunset Park, 455 Sprague Road, Memphis,
(315) 635-6450

KOA, Plainville Road, Plainville, (315) 635-6405

Ice Cream: Available at Beaver Lake Nature Center

Byrne Dairy, Salina Street, Baldwinsville

Trail Directions

- From the visitor center, head north on Deep Woods Trail. A large over-
head sign will direct you to the trailhead and a raised mulch trail bed.
- You'll start in a deciduous forest, then proceed into a pine forest.
- Cross a short boardwalk.
- At the trail junction, turn right on the Lake Loop Trail.
- Walk the boardwalk for about 10 minutes, traversing a swamp area with
lush growth.
- When the boardwalk ends, the trail will be a six-foot-wide mulched path.
Continue on the wide trail, past a trail to the right.
- A second trail to the right leads to a lean-to shelter.
- A trail to the left heads down to water's edge.
- A wood rail fence will be on the right.
- Follow the arrow sign and bear left at a junction with a service road.
- Pass the halfway sign. You've come 1.6 miles.
- Cross another boardwalk for about two minutes.
- Cross a bridge.
- An observation platform with a scope will be on the right, accessible
from Vann Road.
- Cross a driveway.
- At the next trail junction turn right onto Three Meadows Trail. (The
name was recently changed from Teal Marsh Trail because the
marshes are drying up in a normal process of succession. Some signs
and maps still show the old name.)
- A small pond is on your right.
- Emerge from the woods into a meadow area.
- Cross a small boardwalk.
- The trail returns to mulch and you may miss the cool cover of the woods
canopy if the sun is out.
- Re-enter the woods.
- Leave the woods after a bench.
- The arboretum will be on the right. (This 0.3 mile loop of mowed-grass

trails takes you through a "tree garden" where a variety of trees are labeled for your enjoyment and study. A box with guides to the arboretum is at the entrance.)

• Pass a pavilion on the left as you approach the parking area and visitor center.

Date Hiked: _____

Notes:

The Erie Canal

The idea for the Erie Canal was born in our very own Finger Lakes area –
in Canandaigua, to be more precise. In the Canandaigua jail, which at the
time was the second floor of Sheriff Elijah Tilloson's hotel, to be absolutely
accurate. The prisoner who dared to dream this grand folly was Jesse
Hawley, a once wealthy businessman besieged with debt from his less than
lucrative freight forwarding business. Hawley had attempted to make a
business out of moving flour and wheat from farms in the area to the
Mynderse Mill at the falls on the Seneca River (now Seneca Falls), then to
market in New York City. The land and water route available to him was
difficult, dangerous, and costly.

Using maps in the Canandaigua jail, Hawley sketched the route for a
man-made waterway linking Lake Erie to the Hudson River. He wrote
fourteen articles detailing the concept, benefits, route, and cost for an idea
many ridiculed as "the effusions of a maniac."

In 1809 a member of the Ontario County legislature took the articles to
Albany for investigation. New York City Mayor Dewitt Clinton took up the
cause. The canal became his political passion when he became governor of
New York.

Ground was broken for the Erie Canal in 1817. Eight years later the canal
opened. American ingenuity overcame a multitude of obstacles along the
way. America had no engineers or engineering schools in the early 1800s.
Clinton asked a British engineer to head this project but he declined the
offer, forcing Clinton to use American leadership. The closest America had
were lawyers with some surveying experience. The canal became a huge on-
the-job-training endeavor. It led to the development of the Rensselaer
Polytechnic Institute in Troy, the Civil Engineering Department of Union
College, and the Rochester Institute of Technology.

These inexperienced engineers had to devise ways to build locks, including ones to overcome the 60-foot rise of the Niagara Escarpment in
Lockport. They had to develop waterproof cement, blast through bedrock,
and build aqueducts, including the 804-foot span over the Genesee River
in downtown Rochester and the 1-mile span over the Irondequoit Valley in
Pittsford. A challenge for the western end of the canal was how to keep
enough water in the canal, especially during summer droughts. To accom-

plish this, feeders were built, rerouting water from lakes, streams, and reservoirs along the way into the canal.

Clinton's Folly – the original Erie Canal – was only 40 feet wide and 4 feet deep. But it was an instant economic success. It shortened the transportation of goods between Buffalo and New York City from six weeks to 10 days and lowered the cost of transporting one ton of freight from $100 to $10. Suddenly goods could move east to market and immigrants could move west to open land. Business boomed.

By 1835 the canal was log jammed with too much traffic and a major effort was undertaken to enlarge it. Locks were doubled to allow two-way traffic and lengthened to accommodate longer boats. In places the canal was straightened to decrease its total length, widened to 70 feet, and deepened to seven feet. This second version of the Erie Canal is now known as the enlarged Erie Canal.

Over the years additional work was done. In some areas there was a second enlarged Erie Canal. But the next major change came in 1918. The canal was once again over capacity. By now technological know-how had improved and engineers knew how to incorporate the canal into existing rivers and control the water levels. The Erie Canal was once again enlarged and moved. This time it took over riverbeds such as the Clyde River and the Mohawk River. The new and improved version was renamed the Barge Canal.

In sections, such as from Lockport to Greece and Fairport to Palmyra, there is little difference in location of the three canals. With each enhancement the ditch simply got larger. In other places the three waterways had distinctly different locations and all three can be seen today. The stretch from Port Byron through Jordan to Camillus is an example of the latter.

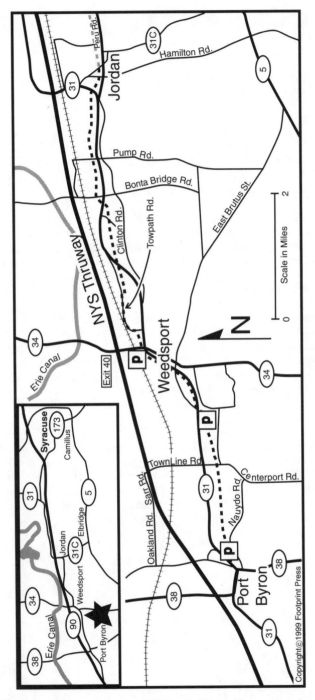

Cayuga County Erie Canal Trail (Port Byron to Jordan)

42.
Cayuga County Erie Canal Trail
(Port Byron to Jordan)

Location: Port Byron, Weedsport, and Jordan (south of the
                 N.Y.S. Thruway), Cayuga and Onondaga Counties
Directions: From Port Byron, head east on Route 31. Park in the
                 canal bed at Randolph J. Schasel Village Park on the
                 south side of Route 31. A small brown and yellow sign,
                 "Cayuga County Erie Canal Trail," is visible from the
                 road.
Alternative Parking: Centerport Aqueduct Park, Route 31, west of
                 Weedsport
                 North Main Street, Jordan, in front of Lock 51 Garden
Hiking Time: 5 hours
Length: 9.3 miles one way
Difficulty:

Surface: Dirt, gravel, and grass trail
Trail Markings: Some signs "Cayuga County Erie Canal Trail"
Uses:

Dogs: OK
Admission: Free
Contact: Tom Higgins, County Planner
                 Cayuga County Planning Board
                 160 Genesee Street
                 Auburn, NY 13021-1276
                 (315) 253-1276

                 Michele Beilman
                 Cayuga County Parks and Trails Commission
                 East Lake Road
                 Auburn, N.Y. 13021
                 (315) 253-5611

205

The 1.5 miles of enlarged Erie Canal that remain between Port Byron and Centerport were made accessible to the public in the fall of 1987. The Lock 52 Historical Society and concerned community members cleared the former towpath and canal bed to make the canal with its hand-placed stone sides visible.

The Randolph J. Schasel Village Park in Port Byron marks the beginning of this trail. It's built partly in the old canal bed and includes a pavilion, playground, and basketball court. Once past Centerport, this trail becomes pretty rough. The trail bed includes gravel, mowed grass, weeds, and some roads. It continues through Weedsport to Jordan. The trail actually continues another 14.8 miles through Erie Canal Park in Camillus. See Trails #43 and #45.

Weedsport derived its name from the Weed brothers, Edward and Elihu, who dug and founded Weed's Basin, a re-supply point on the original Erie Canal.

Bed and Breakfast: The Mansard B&B, Weedsport, (315) 834-2262

Campgrounds: Hejamada Family RV Park, RD 1 McDonald Road, Port Byron, (315) 776-5887

Riverforest Park, 2526 Riverforest Road, Weedsport, (315) 834-9458

Trail Directions
- From the parking area, head east on the trail between Route 31 and the basketball court. The abandoned enlarged Erie Canal will be on your right. Further to the right is the original Clinton's Ditch.
- At 0.9 mile, pass the Harring Brook receiver. All the water from this creek dumped into the canal.
- Cross Centerport Road.
- Cross a wooden bridge. Centerport Aqueduct will be on the right. It was built in 1835 to carry the canal over Cold Spring Brook. There is a rare dam in the creek next to the aqueduct.
- At 2.4 miles, reach Centerport Aqueduct Park and Route 31. Parking is available here.
- Turn right and follow Route 31 for 1.5 miles to Route 34.
- Cross Route 31 to Arby's. The trail continues behind Arby's.
- Pass the brown sign for "Cayuga County Erie Canal Trail."
- Cross a wooden bridge over Putnum Brook, then pass a pond and pen,

home to ducks, geese, turkeys, and chickens.
- At 4.1 miles, reach Towpath Road and turn left on the road.
- Follow Towpath Road for 0.7 mile. The trail begins again on the right after a chained gate into the back of Cayuga County Fairgrounds. There are no signs and no parking area, simply a mowed-grass path heading southeast.
- Turn right onto the trail. You're in a pleasant woods tunnel with the old canal to your left and a creek to your right.
- At 5.6 miles, cross Route 31 and bear left. (The snowmobile trail to the right returns to Weedsport, Route 31B.)
- The trail will get rough. Watch carefully for woodchuck holes.
- Cross Lippoldt Road.
- At 6.5 miles, cross Route 31 again.
- Cross Bonta Bridge Road. The trail bed will improve.
- Cross Pump Road. The abandoned canal is again on your right.
- Pass a double lock from the abandoned enlarged Erie Canal on your right.
- Cross a farm lane. The trail turns from gravel to dirt with roots.
- At 8.7 miles, cross Route 31. The trail continues in the woods behind a sign, "Jordan-Elbridge Area Church Board."
- Cross through a mowed field. The back of the Jordan Diner will be to your left.
- Cross Werner Way, then cross the grass behind the fire hall.
- Cross Hamilton Road.
- Immediately in front of you will be a park. Cross the park on the mowed grass inside the old canal bed until you reach North Main Street, Jordan. (Parking is available along North Main Street.) You've come 9.3 miles.
  [Continue straight on the path between Lock 51 Garden and the Masonic Lodge to connect with the Erie Canalway Trail #43 (Jordan to Camillus), for a 20-mile walk.]

Date Hiked: _____
Notes:

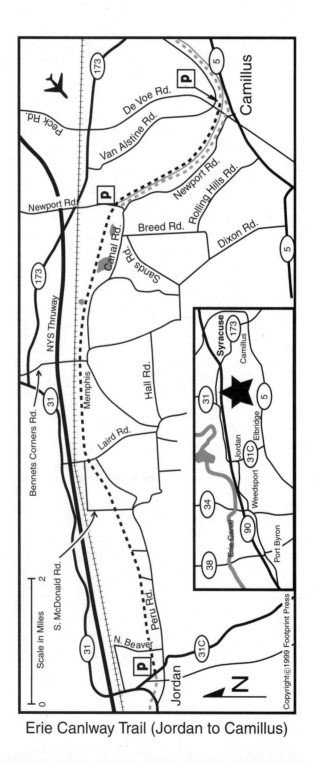

Erie Canlway Trail (Jordan to Camillus)

43.
Erie Canalway Trail (Jordan to Camillus)

Location: Jordan to Camillus, Onondaga County
Directions: Park along North Main Street (Route 31C), Jordan, in
                    front of Lock 51 Garden (between the laundromat and
                    Masonic Lodge).
Alternative Parking: Town of Camillus Erie Canal Park, Newport Road
                    Camillus Erie Canal Park, DeVoe Road
Hiking Time: 5.5 hours
Length: 10.8 miles one way
Difficulty: 🥾
                    🥾

Surface: Dirt and gravel trail
Trail Markings: None
Uses: 🚶 🚴 🎿 🛷

Dogs: OK
Admission: Free
Contact: P.O. Box 397
                    Jordan, NY 13080
                    (315) 689-3278

Also called the Erie Canal Parkway, this is an easy to follow, well-maintained trail along the abandoned enlarged Erie Canal.

Trail Directions
- Head east along the path between Lock 51 Garden and the Masonic Lodge.
- Pass North Beaver Street as you ride through Old Erie Place Park. Picnic tables and parking are available here.
- The enlarged Erie Canal will appear on your

In Jordan, the abandoned canal bed is now a park.

right.
- Pass a road on the right.
- Pass Schapp Road.
- Reach the waste weir on the left. This is where water from Carpenter Brook was used to help control the level of water in the enlarged Erie Canal.
- Cross South McDonald Road in Peru.
- Pass a private house and the McIntyre, a former hotel along the canal, as you approach Laird Road. You've gone 4.2 miles.

West of Jordan, the abandoned canal still holds water.

- At 5.8 miles, cross Bennets Corners Road at the town of Memphis.
- Cross under power lines.
- Pass a gravel road to the right. The trail becomes a gravel and paved roadway.
- At 8.6 miles, cross Newport Road. The Brown Cow Café is on this corner. Across the road, enter the Town of Camillus Erie Canal Project. (Parking is available here.)
- Pass the Camillus Sportsman's Club.
- Cross Devoe Road into Camillus Erie Canal Park. (Parking is available here.) You've come 10.8 miles.
  [Continue to Erie Canal Park Trail #45 for an additional 2.9 mile loop.]

Date Hiked: _____

Notes:

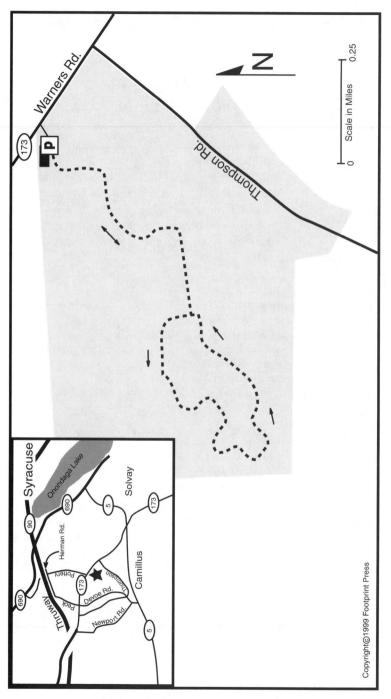

Camillus Forest Unique Area

44.
Camillus Forest Unique Area

Location: 8 miles west of Syracuse, Onondaga County
Directions: From N.Y.S. Thruway exit 39, head south on Herman
                 Road and Pottery Road to Route 173. Take Route 173
                 (Warners Road) south. Camillus Forest Unique Area is
                 accessed from the west side of Route 173. Follow the
                 driveway to the boarded-up school building and park in
                 front of the yellow and green sign, "Parking Area."

Alternative Parking: None
Hiking Time: 1.5 hour
Length: 2 mile loop
Difficulty: 👣 👣 👣

Surface: Mowed tractor path and dirt trails
Trail Markings: 2-inch round yellow plastic "Foot Trail Markers"
Uses: 🥾

Dogs: Pets NOT allowed
Admission: Free
Contact: N.Y.S. Department of Environmental Conservation
                 1285 Fisher Avenue
                 Cortland, NY 13045-1090
                 (607) 753-3095
                 http://www.dec.state.ny.us

D.E.C. calls this a unique area and it is truly unique and special. It comprises 145 acres of open fields, 135 acres of early successional trees and shrubs, 38 acres of old forest, 18 acres of mature sugar maple, American beech, and bitternut hickory, and 13 acres of riparian zone. The trail follows a long, gradual uphill tractor path through fields to a stand of nearly old growth forest. Although old, this forest is not undisturbed pre-settlement "old growth" forest. The stand was harvested in the distant past, and may have been managed as a sugar bush for maple sap production. However, given the dignity of time, this forest will give us a glimpse of the transition from "old forest" to "old growth forest."

Within the old forest are several very large sugar maples, New York State's official tree. American beech can be found with diameters at breast height exceeding 36 inches. Estimated age of eleven of the dominant trees in the forest is between 120 and 200 years, with one 42-inch sugar maple tree approaching 300 years of age.

Sarah and John Vacher originally settled this land in 1796. In 1810 the Hopkins family acquired the property and continued to farm the area until the late 1880s. Agricultural statistics from 1855 describe the land as cropland, pasture, and meadow. Crops grown included potatoes, winter wheat, oats, corn, and barley. Sheep, swine, and milking cows were the dominant livestock. The 1821 Camillus census indicates that sheep significantly outnumbered other livestock, and the town produced immense quantities of wool. The Erie Canal, which opened in 1825, provided transportation for grains and wool.

Camillus Forest Unique Area was purchased by New York State in 1926. It was administered by the Syracuse Developmental Center until March 1997 when Governor George E. Pataki transferred stewardship to the D.E.C.

Within the old forest, two-inch round, blue tags are affixed to trees. Watch carefully for them at eye level. Here is the description for each tag, as provided by D.E.C.:

#1 Edge of the old forest: Congratulations! You have reached the old forest portion of the unique area. The large trees you see are sugar maple, with an occasional bitternut hickory or basswood. Sugar maple is valued for many reasons. It provides shade, sap for maple syrup, den and nesting cavities for wildlife, gives us beautiful fall color, as well as wood for flooring, furniture, and bowling pins. Like all trees, sugar maple produces oxygen, removes carbon dioxide from the environment, filters dust and absorbs noise; its roots help stabilize soils, thereby reducing sedimentation and enhancing water quality. Sugar maple requires fertile, moist soil conditions for optimum growth. It is not suited to stressful environments and is not salt tolerant, thereby making it a poor choice for planting in urban areas or along major highways.

#2 Old grader, early 1900s: This old grader was horse-drawn and probably utilized to construct farm roads. Look at plants on the ground; you will find maple leaved waterleaf, eastern waterleaf, and touch-me-not in great

213

quantities along with occasional rock piles created by settlers clearing the land.

The horse-drawn grader found in Camillus Forest.

#3 Old stump: The cutting of this tree provided light to the forest floor and opportunities for shade-tolerant sugar maple saplings to become established in the forest understory. The trees one to two inches in diameter are nearly 40 years old. This is because they are heavily shaded, and are growing very slowly. Sugar maple has the ability to increase in growth once additional light is made available. Look at the forest floor, you will find Christmas ferns and blue cohosh, a plant that is an indicator of rich, limestone-based soils. You will also note a slippery or red elm, with sprouts coming from the trunk. These sprouts suggest that the tree is in decline and lacking vigor.

#4 Small natural forest opening: You have just passed through the only section of forest that has black cherry, a relatively fast-growing, shade-intolerant (light-loving) tree that belongs to the rose family. Black cherry is readily identifiable by its cornflake-like rough-textured black bark. It requires openings greater than a half acre in size to become established. This stop illustrates a natural forest opening that was created when a sugar maple and bitternut were blown down by wind. Seedlings and saplings are taking advantage of light, heat, and nutrients provided by this opening.

Herbaceous and woody vegetation provides valuable browse for white-tailed deer. Red elderberry, wild leek, and American basswood can be found. Openings or lateral gaps in the canopy are typically found in forests that are developing into old growth. Spring wildflowers found in the forest include Dutchman's breeches, toothwort, purple trillium, white trillium, false Solomon's seal, yellow forest violet, and Carolina spring beauty. Initial plant surveys found nearly 80 different plants in this forest.

#5 Large natural forest opening: Along this segment of trail you will see a significant forest opening in the process of development. Look up at the sky and across the opening; you will see large gaps between trees and standing dead (snag) trees, some of which provide dens and cavities for wildlife such as raccoon, gray squirrel, saw-whet owl, screech owl, pileated woodpecker, and yellow shafted flicker. Insects associated with snags also provide food for wildlife. Take a minute to look and listen. You will likely hear the call of wood thrush, veery, yellow-shafted flicker, or blue jay. Birds that migrate from the tropics (neotropical migrants) such as the scarlet tanager have been observed in this forest opening as well.

#6 Decaying tree: As you walk through the forest you will find remnants of old trees, referred to by foresters as coarse woody debris. Once a tree dies, it decays and nutrients are recycled back into the soil. Here you see a tree that fell over between 10 and 15 years ago. As you walk through the forest, notice other trees that have tipped over along with portions of their root systems. As old trees tip over and decay, hummocks are created on the forest floor by the soil piles left, creating the hummock and hollow "micro topography" found in older forests. Soils in this forest are classified as chiefly Camillus, Ontario, and Hilton loams, soils that have a high natural limestone, red sandstone, and shale. These soils are very productive from a forestry standpoint. Even so, most tree roots are no deeper than 24 to 36 inches, as the roots need to exchange oxygen and carbon dioxide. Find a recently blown over tree along the trail; see how small the root system is on these large trees.

#7 Largest sugar maple trees: You are entering the portion of the forest with the largest number of giant sugar maple trees. Next to you is a 38-inch sugar maple that sheep or cattle may have once grazed around. It was a common practice for farmers to allow grazing in the forest as it prevented the forest understory from growing, thereby keeping the forest "park-like" and making activities such as firewood cutting or sugar maple sap collection easier.

#8 Largest sugar maple: This sugar maple is the largest and oldest in the forest, with an estimated age of 285 years (approximately birth date of 1712) and height of 110 feet. Maximum tree heights approach 126 feet in the forest. Note the shaggy bark, an indication of how old this tree is. Over its entire life, this tree has grown at an approximate rate of 14 rings to the inch. The average growth of young to moderately aged healthy sugar maples that are codominant to dominant in the forest canopy in Central New York is 10 rings to the inch, or two inches in a decade.

#9 Old broken American beech: American beech produces beechnuts (hard mast) for wildlife such as the blue jay, turkey, and deer. Unfortunately, Central New York beech is dying due to beech bark scale complex, a fungus disease that eventually girdles and kills the tree. Butternut canker has killed the majority of trees in this forest stand as well. Analysis of trees over six inches in diameter shows that 83% of the forest is sugar maple and 13% is American beech. Most of the American beech will die within the next 20 to 30 years due to age and disease, providing opportunities for a new generation of trees.

#10 Exit the woods: Feel the change in temperature (depending on the season) as you exit the "big woods." On a clear day you see well into neighboring Oswego, Madison, and Oneida counties to the Tug Hill Plateau and Mohawk River valley. Look for songbirds, butterflies, turkey, deer, and an occasional coyote as you wind back to the trailhead.

Trail Directions
- From the parking area, head west on the trail past trail markers.
- The trail winds through fields on a tractor path and heads uphill to great valley views.
- Cross the mowed field and continue uphill. (Markers will be sporadic through this section.)
- Reach a "T" with trail markers and turn right.
- At 0.9 mile, enter the woods. Follow the yellow markers carefully through the woods. Many other paths intersect.
- Exit the woods. Spectacular valley views await you. Notice Oneida Lake in the distance.
- Reach the trail junction and turn right (E), heading downhill all the way to the parking area.

Date Hiked: _____
Notes:

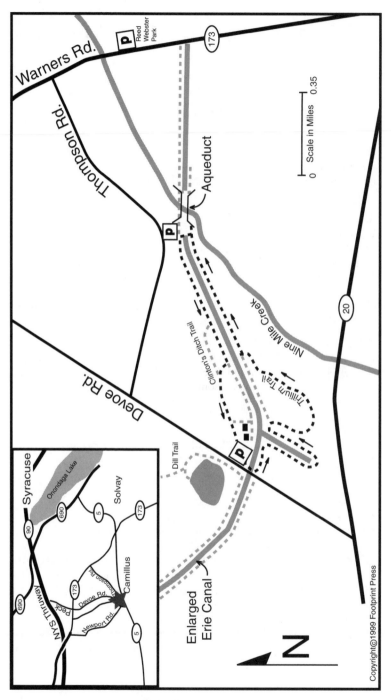

Erie Canal Park

45.
Erie Canal Park

Location: Camillus (west of Syracuse), Onondaga County
Directions: From Route 5, turn north on Devoe Road. Erie Canal
                   Park is on the right, just south of Thompson Road.
Alternative Parking: A parking area off Thompson Road, near the dock
                   and aqueduct
Hiking Time: 1.5 hours
Length: 2.9 mile loop
Difficulty: 👟 👟
                   👟 👟
Surface: Dirt and gravel trail
Trail Markings: None
Uses: 🚶 🥾

Dogs: OK on leash
Admission: Free
Contact: Town of Camillus Erie Canal Park
                   David Beebe, Director Sims' Museum
                   109 East way
                   Camillus, NY 13031
                   (315) 488-3409

                   Camillus Town Hall
                   4600 West Genesee Street
                   Syracuse, NY 13219
                   (315) 488-1234

The enlarged Erie Canal was abandoned in 1922, then sat idle until 1972 when the town of Camillus purchased a seven-mile stretch. Since then an army of volunteers has been busy clearing the land, building dams, refilling the canal with water, and building a replica of Sims' store. The original Sims' store was built in 1856 at the intersection of Warners Road and the canal. It served as a general store, home for the Sims family, and departure point for people boarding the canal boats. The store was destroyed by fire in 1863, the replica lives on today. The first floor is setup like the original store. The second floor houses exhibits and antiques of the era along with models of locks, aqueducts, and canal boats. Sims' Museum is open Saturdays year-round from 9:00 AM until 1:00 PM, and Sundays from

218

1:00 PM until 5:00 PM, May through October, and 1:00 PM to 4:00 PM, November through April.

The trails are available year-round during daylight hours. This trail circumnavigates the historic enlarged Erie Canal and parallels sections of the original Clinton's Ditch. It also takes you to view the remains of the aqueduct which once carried the canal waters over Nine Mile Creek. Rain shelters are built at several locations along the trail.

Walking the towpath of the aqueduct over Nine Mile Creek.

To extend your walk, there is an additional 0.5 mile loop from the Sims' Museum on the Dill Trail. Dill's Landing was once a wide waters and boat slip along Clinton's Ditch. Cross Devoe Road and take a quick right onto the trail. The trail will "Y" with the left leading to a view of the pond and the right leading past interpretive signs to the stone-lined cavity of the old boat slip.

Bed & Breakfasts:	B&B Wellington, 707 Danforth Street, Syracuse, (315) 474-3641
	Green Gate Inn, 2 Genesee Street, Camillus, (315) 672-9276
Boat Tour:	Canal Boat Tours are offered Sundays, May through October, from 1:00 PM until 5:00 PM. Cost is

219

$1.50 children, $3 adults. Dinner cruises are also offered. Call (315) 488-3409 for details.

Ice Cream: Village of Camillus Sunoco Gas Station, corner Main Street (West Genesee Street) and Newport Road (seasonal)

Trail Directions

The boathouse at Erie Canal Park.

- From the parking area at Sims' store, walk west toward Devoe Road. Just before the road, turn left and cross a wooden bridge.
- Turn left (E) onto the path on the opposite side of the canal.
- At the pedestrian bridge, turn right on the West Feeder Trail.
- Reach the end of the feeder and turn left around its end to return on the opposite side.
- Reach the canal and turn right (E).
- Reach the entrance to Trillium Trail and turn right.
- Cross three wooden bridges as this trail winds through the woods.
- At 0.9 mile, you'll reach the canal again. Turn right.
- Reach the dock at 1.6 miles. (A parking area is to the left on Thompson Road.) Continue straight to a dead end at the aqueduct. All that remains are the stone supports for the wooden trough and the towpath.
- Turn around and walk back to the dock.
- Turn right, then a quick left, to continue walking on the other side of the canal, now heading west.
- Pass a trail to the right.
- At 2.3 miles, turn right at the sign for "Culvert #59." This culvert carried runoff water under the canal to Nine Mile Creek.
- Cross a long wooden bridge, then head uphill to parallel the original Clinton's Ditch.
- Continue on the trail to the parking area at Sims' Museum.

Date Hiked: _____
Notes:

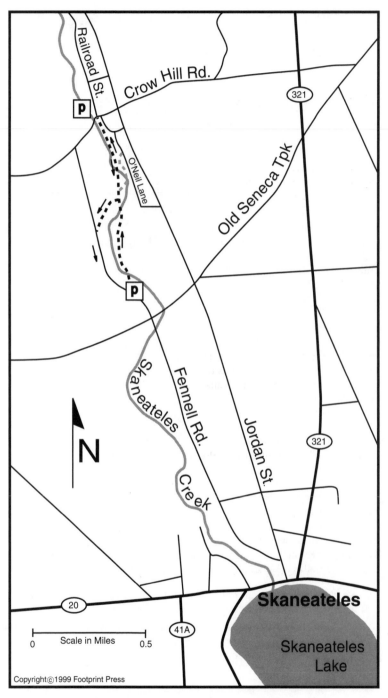

Charlie Major Nature Trail

46.
Charlie Major Nature Trail

Location: North of the village of Skaneateles, Onondaga County
Directions: From Route 20 in Skaneateles, turn north onto Jordan
                      Street, then left onto Fennell Road. Look for a gravel
                      parking area 500-feet north of Old Seneca Turnpike on
                      the right (E) side of Fennel Road. A gray sign with
                      black lettering, "Nature Trail," marks the area.
Alternative Parking: A parking area on Crow Hill Road near the corner of
                      Railroad Street.
Hiking Time: 50 minutes
Length: 1.6 mile loop
Difficulty:

Surface: Dirt and crushed stone trail
Trail Markings: None
Uses:

Dogs: OK
Admission: Free
Contact: Town of Skaneateles
                      24 Jordan Street
                      Skaneateles, NY 13152
                      (315) 685-3473

The Charlie Major Nature Trail was named after Charles T. Major Jr., a
public figure who featured prominently in the history and development of
this rail trail. Major served as village justice, town justice, town board member, and town supervisor from the 1950s through the 1990s, often taking
town employees on nature walks to this obscure place in the area's history.
The nature trail was his idea. Today he is a state supreme court justice.

The early settlers, arriving in the area from 1794 on, saw that the drop of
100 feet in the flow of water down the Skaneateles outlet from Skaneateles
Lake north would furnish waterpower for industry. This cheap source of
waterpower gave rise to the bustling community of Mottville. A railroad for

horse-drawn cars was built along the creek in 1840, to be followed by a plank road which was used only a few years. This was followed by the steam railroad in 1866. Mills dotted the waterfront. They included sawmills, gristmills, tanneries, woolen mills, distilleries, and paper mills. As these industries declined, their factories became sites for the manufacture of vacuum cleaners, cement blocks, tiles, chemicals, and medical instruments.

Remains of a dam from Mottville Woodworking Factory.

Remains of this industrial era can be seen along the trail today. Parts of the dam and headrace from Mottville Woodworking Factory are on the side trail heading up to O'Neil Lane. This factory was originally a power plant, then a woodworking factory that made tools for farmers in 1826. Also visible are stone ruins from Morton's Woolen Mill, which began in 1800 as a sawmill, gristmill, and distillery. It was built into a factory in 1852. In 1862 it made uniforms for Union soldiers under the name Mottville Woolen Mill. The mill closed in 1890 and burned in 1894.

When the city of Syracuse began using the water from Skaneateles Lake for its drinking water, it took over control of the dam at the outlet. The water level in the creek was lowered below a level necessary for mill operations, so other methods of power generation had to be sought. At one point, so little water flowed down the Skaneateles outlet that the sewage concentration became high enough to instigate a breakout of typhoid. A second epidemic swept the area in the 1920s when well water became contaminated. Charles Major Sr., organized a town committee to bring piped water to the community.

The rail line, eventually known as the Short Line, helped maintain prosperity in the community by serving the industries along the outlet. It also carried passengers from the New York Central Railroad at Skaneateles Junction to Skaneateles where they could board steamboats for trips around the lake. Today the rails are gone and a serene path follows Skaneateles Creek for part of its journey as it flows northward from

223

Skaneateles Lake into the Seneca River. The trail is equally pleasant as a walk or bike ride.

Bed & Breakfasts: Fox Ridge Farm B&B, Skaneateles, (315) 673-4881

The Gray House, 47 Jordan Street, Skaneateles, (315) 685-5224

Hobbit Hollow Farm B&B, 3061 West Lake Road, Skaneateles, (315) 685-2791

Lady of the Lake B&B, 2 West Lake Street, Skaneateles, (888) 685-7997

Millard's at the Summit B&B, Route 41, Skaneateles, (315) 673-2254

Sherwood Inn, 26 West Genesee Street, Skaneateles, (315) 685-3405

Trail Directions
- From the parking area on Fennel Road, head northwest on the trail.
- Cross a wooden bridge over Skaneateles Creek.
- The creek will now be on your left, parallel to the trail.
- Cross a second bridge.
- At 0.3 mile, reach a "Y" intersection. (The trail to the left goes for 0.12 mile to Fennel Road.) Continue straight (S).
- Immediately after a brick shed is a trail to the right. Notice the dam in the creek to the right. (The trail to the right heads uphill for 0.13 mile to O'Neil Lane past the dam and crosses a mill race.) Continue straight.
- At 0.5 mile, cross a bridge over the creek.
- Reach Crow Hill Road at 0.8 mile. Turn around and walk back on the same path.
- When the trail "Ys," bear right.
- Turn left onto Fennel Road and walk the road back to the parking area.

Date Hiked: _____
Notes:

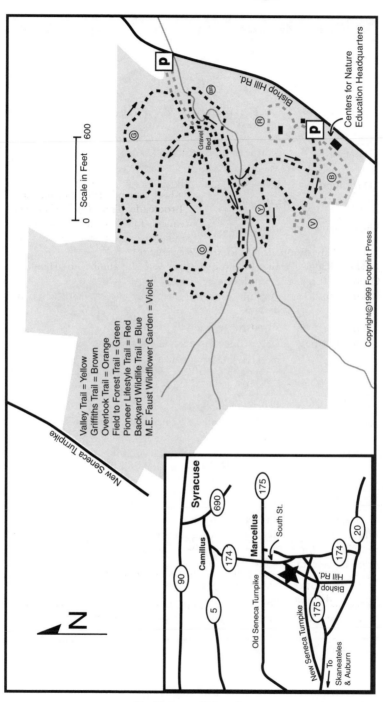

Valley Trail = Yellow
Griffiths Trail = Brown
Overlook Trail = Orange
Field to Forest Trail = Green
Pioneer Lifestyle Trail = Red
Backyard Wildlife Trail = Blue
M.E. Faust Wildflower Garden = Violet

Centers for Nature
Education Headquarters

Bishop Hill Rd.

New Seneca Turnpike

0   Scale in Feet   600

Gravel
Bed

Copyright©1999 Footprint Press

Syracuse

690

175

Camillus

174

Marcellus

South St.

174

20

90

5

Old Seneca Turnpike

New Seneca Turnpike

Bishop Hill Rd.

175

174

To
Skaneateles
& Auburn

N

Baltimore Woods

47.
Baltimore Woods

Location: Northeast of Skaneateles Lake in the town of
                 Marcellus, Onondaga County
Directions: From Skaneateles, take Route 20 east, then Route 175
                 east. Turn left (N) on Bishop Hill Road. The upper
                 parking area for Baltimore Woods will be on the left
                 (W) at the top of the hill.
Alternative Parking: Lower parking area also on Bishop Hill Road
Hiking Time: 1.75 hours
Length: 2.5 mile loop
Difficulty: 🥾 🥾 🥾

Surface: Wood-chipped and dirt trails
Trail Markings: Color-coded signposts and some plastic and wooden
                 markers, and paint blazes
Uses: 🚶 ♿

Dogs: Pets NOT allowed
Admission: A $2 per person or $3 per family donation is
                 suggested.
Contact: Centers for Nature Education, Inc.
                 P.O. Box 133, 4007 Bishop Hill Road
                 Marcellus, NY 13108-0133
                 (315) 673-1350

Eight loop trails cover this 170-acre nature center which is owned by Save the County, Inc. (a local non-profit land trust), and managed and operated by Centers for Nature Education, Inc. (a non-profit environmental education organization). Each trail is color-coded and easy-to-follow.

The route described wanders around the outside perimeter of four of the trails in the following order:

Yellow – Valley Trail: A 0.6 mile loop down the glacial valley and across Baltimore Brook.

Orange – Overlook Trail: A 0.7 mile hike over glacial mounds.

The log cabin at Baltimore Woods.

Brown – Griffiths Trail: A 0.3 mile meander through the active flood plain of Baltimore Brook.

Green – Field to Forest Trail: A 0.7 mile traverse of rolling terrain through woods and fields. The mature forest was once a sugarbush.

Four easy trails near the parking area are not included in the route described below. They are:

Blue – Backyard Wildlife Trail: A 0.3 mile loop on level ground which winds through plantings for wildlife and is handicapped accessible.

Red – Pioneer Lifestyle Trail: A 0.3 mile loop encircling the pioneer homestead area.

Violet – Mildred E. Faust Wildflower Garden: A 0.3 mile maze through labeled plantings of native wildflowers and ferns.

Extension – Harrison Loop: A 0.25 mile trail that enters the wooded area surrounding Faust Garden for nature studies.

Trail Directions

- From the upper parking area, walk behind the pavilion on a wood-chipped trail, heading toward the yellow trail.
- Pass labeled flowerbeds.
- Enter the woods and head downhill to the valley bottom.
- Cross Baltimore Brook on a wooden bridge.
- At the intersection, turn left (W) on the orange trail.
- Cross Baltimore Brook again on a wooden bridge.
- Immediately after the brook, turn right to stay on the orange trail along

227

the brook.
- Cross another bridge, then climb out of the valley.
- Reach a trail to the left. A short side trip leads to an overlook point.
- Back on the main trail, reach a junction and turn left (NE).
- Follow a split rail fence along the edge of a clearing.
- At one point, a tree trunk lined path leads right to an observation point overlooking the valley. The orange trail bends left.
- Pass a small trail on the left.
- Reach the intersection with the yellow trail and turn left (E).
- At the next intersection, continue straight (E) on the brown trail.
- Soon, reach another intersection and continue straight (E) on the brown trail.
- Soon reach another intersection and continue straight (E).
- Continue straight through a junction, past a gravel bed.
- At the next junction, turn left (NW). (Straight goes to the lower parking area.)
- Bear left at a junction and climb a hill.
- Continue straight at a bench, past a trail to the left.
- Head downhill.
- Enter a field. The trail bends right through the field which can be overgrown at times.
- Bear right at a junction past a trail to the left that goes to the lower parking area.
- Reach the junction with another trail to the lower parking area. Turn right onto the brown trail.
- At the next junction, turn left (SE), pass through the gravel bed again, and continue on the brown trail.
- Pass through a shrubby area, then cross a small wooden bridge and head into woods.
- Cross five more small wooden bridges and another field before returning to the woods.
- At the trail junction, turn left (W) onto the yellow trail.
- At the next junction, turn left (S) and head downhill.
- Cross a bridge over Baltimore Brook.
- Climb through a notch in the hills beside a spring-fed stream.
- At a junction, turn left (SE) to return to the upper parking area.

Date Hiked: _____
Notes:

Walks in Tompkins & Cortland Counties

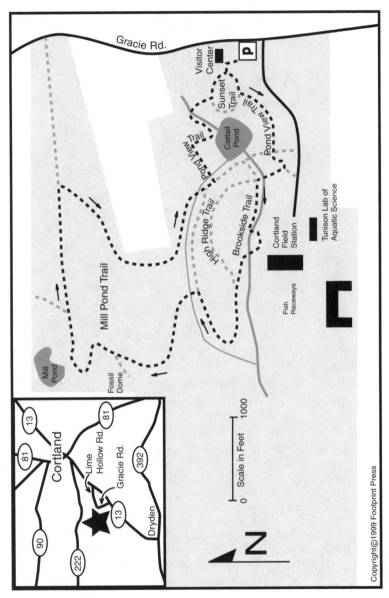

Lime Hollow Nature Center

48.
Lime Hollow Nature Center

Location: Southwest of Cortland, Cortland County
Directions: Follow Route 13 south from Cortland. Turn north on
                     Gracie Road. Parking will be on the west side of Gracie
                     Road at the sign "Tunison Lab of Aquatic Science."
Alternative Parking: None
Hiking Time: 1.5 hours
Length: 3.0 mile loop
Difficulty: 🥾 🥾 🥾

Surface: Dirt trails
Trail Markings: Color-coded, geometric-shaped trail markers on posts
Uses: 🚶 🎿

Dogs: OK on leash
Admission: Free
Contact: Lime Hollow Nature Center
                     3091 Gracie Road
                     Cortland, NY 13045-9355
                     (607) 758-5462

Lime Hollow Nature Center covers 115 acres of diverse woodlands with five loop trails available for hiking. There is a visitor center with interpretive exhibits and live animal exhibits. It also offers restrooms, a water fountain, and a picnic area. The visitor center is open Monday through Saturday from 9:00 AM to 5:00 PM and Sunday from 1:00 PM to 4:00 PM.

Fossil Dome is a unique feature of Lime Hollow Nature Center. Off Mill Pond Trail, it's a site where many fossils can be found. Another unique feature is the Tunison Lab of Aquatic Science, which is open to visitors. Salmon, rainbow, and lake trout can be seen in indoor and outdoor raceways.

The trails are well marked with signs coded by color and geometric shape:

Lime Hollow trails are well marked.

Sunset Trail (white diamonds) is 0.3 mile long. It winds through the conifer plantation near the visitor center and features interpretive signs about LHNC and nature.

Pondview Trail (yellow circles) circles Cattail Pond for 0.85 mile and offers a view of many different kinds of wetland plants and animals.

Brookside Trail (red triangles) wanders for 1.0 mile through a coniferous forest and passes the Tunison Lab of Aquatic Science trout viewing area.

High Ridge Trail (blue squares) gradually climbs to Hemlock Overlook. It is a 0.25 mile long glacial esker.

Mill Pond Trail (orange hexagons) heads to the farthest section of Lime Hollow Nature Center and leads to Fossil Dome. It's a 1.5 mile trail through mixed hardwood forest.

The route described here is a clockwise outer loop incorporating all the trails. It's a hilly walk through the woods.

Lime Hollow Nature Center recently purchased an additional 190 acres adjacent to their current location. Look for many new trails and exciting programs in the next few years.

Bed & Breakfasts:	The Candlelight Inn, 49 West Main Street, Dryden, (607) 844-4321
	The Copper Iris B&B, 3718 West Road, Route 281, Cortland, (607) 753-3088
	Haven of Rest B&B, 7 Gulf Hill Road, McLean, (607) 838-3722
	The Manor House B&B, 29 Tompkins Street, Cortland, (607) 756-2908
	Serendipity B&B, 15 North Street, Dryden, (607) 844-9589
Campgrounds:	Cortland's Country Music Park, 1804-24 Truxton Road (Route 13), Cortland, (607) 753-0377
	Yellow Lantern, 1770 Truxton Road (Route 13), Cortland, (607) 756-2959

Ice Cream: Purple Lion, 52 North Street, Dryden, (607) 844-9636

Footies Freeze, Tompkins Street Extension, Cortland, (607) 756-8787

A&W Drive-in, junction Routes 13 & 281, Cortland, (607) 756-2021

Trail Directions

- From the parking area, follow the "Trail Entrance" sign to the visitor center building.
- Before the visitor center building, turn left under another "Trail Entrance" sign to begin on Sunset Trail.
- Reach a "Y" and bear left on Pondview Trail (yellow circles) following the sign, "To Tunison Woods Trail."
- Turn right on a gravel road, then a quick left before the barricade. Pass an enclosed spring on the right.
- Cross a small bridge. Turn right to the pond. Tunison Lab will be to the left.
- Cross a small bridge.
- Turn left onto Brookside Trail (red triangles). Follow the red markers across the stream.
- Turn right on the grass. Cross the stream again on a boardwalk.
- Turn left to stay on Brookside Trail.
- Turn left on Mill Pond Trail (orange hexagons).
- Take the short side trail to Fossil Dome, then return to Mill Pond Trail.
- Follow trail markers carefully as Mill Pond Trail turns right. (The access road straight ahead goes to Gracie Road and Chicago Bog.)
- Pass a spring on the right.
- Pass a metal building and bear left on Brookside Trail (red triangles).
- Turn left on Pondview Trail (yellow circles) and cross a boardwalk.
- As the trail heads toward the pond, notice the stack of branches clipped by beavers near shore. The beavers no longer live in this pond.
- Turn left on Sunset Trail (white diamonds).
- Pass the visitor center on your return to the parking area.

Date Hiked: _____
Notes:

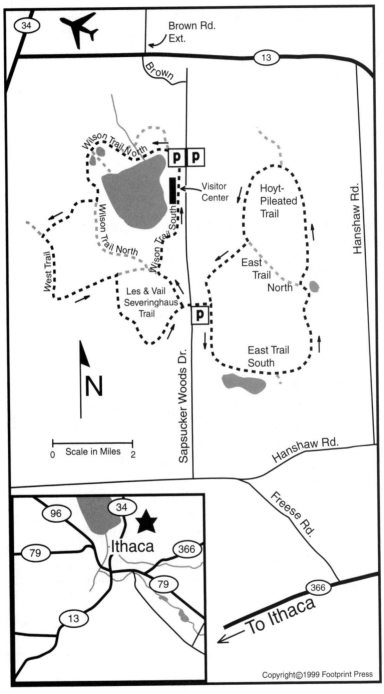

Sapsucker Woods

49.
Sapsucker Woods

Location: East of Ithaca, Tompkins County
Directions: From Route 13, heading east from the south end of
                    Cayuga Lake, turn right (S) on Brown Road Extension.
                    Turn right on Sapsucker Woods Drive. The parking
                    area will be on the right.
Alternative Parking: Two other parking areas on Sapsucker Woods Drive
Hiking Time: 1.25 hours
Length: 2.5 mile loop
Difficulty:

Surface: Mulched trails
Trail Markings: None (some intersections have posted maps)
Uses:

Dogs: Pets NOT allowed
Admission: Free
Contact: Sapsucker Woods
                    Cornell Laboratory of Ornithology
                    159 Sapsucker Woods Drive
                    Ithaca, NY 14851
                    (607) 254-BIRD
                    http://birds.cornell.edu

You won't want to hurry on this trail. The raised mulch foot bed makes for a soft walk as you wander through the woods past ponds. The area is alive with wildlife. Close to the visitor center, the trails have voice boxes. Press a button and you'll learn about the wildlife and vegetation of the area.

The Cornell Lab of Ornithology is open Monday through Thursday 8:00 AM to 5:00 PM, Friday 8:00 AM to 4:00 PM, and Saturday 10:00 AM to 4:00 PM. Trails are always open; simply close the gates behind you. Within the Cornell Lab of Ornithology is the Lyman K. Stuart Observatory, where you can sit and watch birds through a large window overlooking the ten-acre pond and listen to their calls piped in through microphones. The Lab presents Monday evening seminars during spring and fall Cornell semesters

235

Welcome to Sapsucker Woods.
(picture compliments of Finger Lakes Association)

featuring lectures by ornithologists, birders, authors, photographers, and other people who have worked extensively with birds. The Lab also houses a superb collection of bird paintings by famed artist Louis Agassiz Fuertes and an excellent birding shop run by Wild Birds Unlimited.

Bed & Breakfasts:	Hanshaw House, 15 Sapsucker Woods Road, Ithaca, (607) 257-1437
	Hound & Hare, 1031 Hanshaw Road, Ithaca, (607) 257-2821
	Sweet Dreams B&B, 228 Wood Street, Ithaca (607) 272-7727
Boat Tour:	Cayuga Lake Cruises, 704 W. Buffalo Street, Ithaca (800) 951-5901
Campgrounds:	Buttermilk Falls State Park, Route 13, Ithaca, (607) 273-5761
	Robert H. Treman State Park, Route 327, Ithaca, (607) 273-3440
	Spruce Row, 2271 Kraft Road, Ithaca, (607) 387-9225

Outfitter: The Outdoor Store, 206 East State Street, Ithaca, (607) 273-3891

Trail Directions

- From the parking area near the visitor center, pass through the gate on Wilson Trail heading north.
- Bear left, past a trail to the right.
- Reach the pond.
- Continue straight where the small loop trail joins from the right.
- Reach a boardwalk. Turn left for a short walk to an observation platform over the wetlands.
- Turn right at the next intersection.

The boardwalk at Sapsucker Woods.

- Reach a "T" and turn left. (Right goes to a private area.)
- At 0.6 mile, cross a wooden bridge.
- Turn right on the Les & Vail Severinghaus Trail.
- Cross a boardwalk.
- At 1.0 mile, pass a trail to the left. Continue straight across Sapsucker Woods Drive and through the gate on the other side.
- Reach a "T" at 1.1 miles and turn right (S).
- Pass a pond.
- At a "Y," bear left. (The trail straight goes to a bench.)
- Reach a shelter and pond. Check for frogs and turtles on the logs.
- At 1.6 miles bear right at a "Y," then cross a narrow boardwalk.
- Bear left at a "Y." (Right is a service entrance.)
- At 1.9 miles bear right over a boardwalk through a fern-filled swamp.
- At 2.1 miles, reach a "Y" and bear right. Cross Sapsucker Woods Drive and pass through the gates on the other side.
- Turn right at the first junction.
- Bear right at the "Y."
- Cross a boardwalk.
- Pass through a gate and continue straight to the parking area.

Date Hiked: _____
Notes:

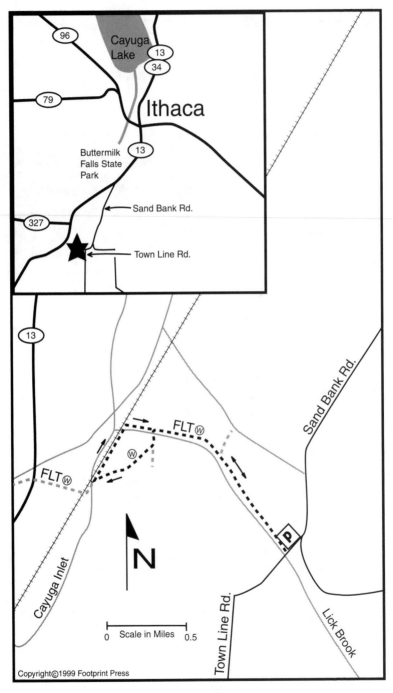

Sweedler Preserve

50.
Sweedler Preserve

Location: South of Ithaca, Tompkins County
Directions: From Ithaca, take Route 13 south. Turn left on Sand
                         Bank Road (the first road past the entrance to
                         Buttermilk Falls State Park). Bear right at the "Y" on
                         Town Line Road. Park on the right side of the road.
Alternative Parking: None
Hiking Time: 1.5 hour
Length: 1.6 mile loop
Difficulty: 🥾 🥾 🥾 🥾
                         🥾 🥾 🥾 🥾

Surface: Dirt and mulch trails
Trail Markings: White blazes
Uses: 🚶

Dogs: OK on leash
Admission: Free
Contact: The Finger Lakes Land Trust
                         202 East Court Street
                         Ithaca, NY 14850
                         (607) 275-9487
                         http://www.cfe.cornell.edu/fllt

                         Finger Lakes Trail Conference
                         P.O. Box 18048
                         Rochester, NY 14618-0048
                         (716) 288-7191
                         http://www.fingerlakes.net/trailsystem

This hike is strenuous. It goes down a steep hill, loops at the bottom, and climbs back up the hill. It's less than two miles but you'll definitely get an aerobic workout. Along the way you'll see waterfalls in the deep gorge of Lick Brook, one of which falls over 140 feet. This is a white-blazed section of the Finger Lakes Trail, a 557-mile-long hiking path that connects the Catskills with the Allegheny Mountains across New York State.

The Finger Lakes Land Trust acquired this unique land through a swap and bargain sale. Owner Moss Sweedler traded his Lick Brook land for a plot with a pond where his dogs could swim. By selling the Lick Brook land for far below market value, Sweedler helped preserve this beautiful land and did us all an immense favor.

Bed & Breakfasts: Hanshaw House, 15 Sapsucker Woods Road, Ithaca, (607) 257-1437

Hound & Hare, 1031 Hanshaw Road, Ithaca, (607) 257-2821

Sweet Dreams B&B, 228 Wood Street, Ithaca (607) 272-7727

Boat Tour: Cayuga Lake Cruises, 704 W. Buffalo Street, Ithaca (800) 951-5901

Campgrounds: Buttermilk Falls State Park, Route 13, Ithaca, (607) 273-5761

Robert H. Treman State Park, Route 327, Ithaca, (607) 273-3440

Spruce Row, 2271 Kraft Road, Ithaca, (607) 387-9225

Outfitters: The Outdoor Store, 206 East State Street, Ithaca, (607) 273-3891

Wildware Outfitters, 171 The Commons, Ithaca, (607) 273-5158

Trail Directions
- From the parking area along Town Line Road, head downhill (W) on the white-blazed trail. Lick Brook will be on your left.
- Cross a small wooden bridge.
- The gully will begin to drop off far below to your left.
- Pass a trail to the right. (It's a short side trail to the next creek bed.)
- The trail now gets steep.
- Pass a lookout to a waterfall.
- At 0.6 mile, reach the brook; the trail levels out.
- Pass a trail to the right.
- Cross Lick Brook. Most of the year the water runs underground at this point.
- Reach an intersection. (Left is a short trail to a stone foundation.)

Continue straight through the field on the white-blazed trail.

• Cross under power lines.

• At 0.8 mile, reach the railroad trestle over Cayuga Inlet. (The white-blazed Finger Lakes Trail turns left to cross the trestle.) Turn right and follow the active Conrail tracks. Watch carefully for trains.

• Immediately after crossing the next bridge, turn right on an unmarked trail.

• Reach a "Y" and bear left, once again on the white-blazed trail.

• At 1.0 mile, begin the half-mile climb to the parking area.

Date Hiked: _____

Notes:

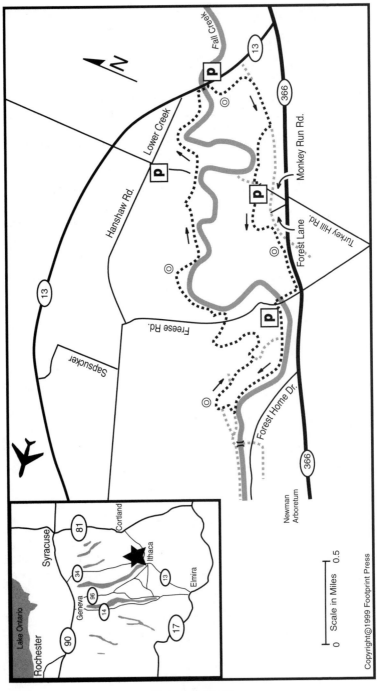

Cayuga Trail

51.
Cayuga Trail

Location:	Ithaca at the south end of Cayuga Lake, Tompkins County
Directions:	From Route 366 (west of the junction with Route 13), turn north on Monkey Run Road. Park at the end of the road, on the left, before the barricade and in front of a sign, "No Parking – Snow Plow Turnaround." Do not park here if it's likely to snow while you're out.
Alternative Parking:	Along the gravel road north of Fall Creek off Freese Road
	At the intersection of Hanshaw Road and Lower Creek Road
	On the east side of Route 13, south of Fall Creek
Hiking Time:	3 hours
Length:	6.5 mile loop
Difficulty:	👣 👣 👣 👣
Surface:	Dirt trails
Trail Markings:	Orange blazes
Uses:	🚶
Dogs:	OK on leash
Admission:	Free
Contact:	Cayuga Trails Club P.O. Box 754 Ithaca, NY 14851-0754

Brothers Richard Hanks, age 11, and Kenneth Hanks, age 14, established portions of this trail in 1945. The area around Fall Creek was called Monkey Run and was popular for hunting, fishing, trapping, and swimming. The Scotch Pine grove you'll hike through was planted with defective European stock and never did particularly well. The abandoned rail bed you'll walk carried coal to the Cornell University heating plant in the 1940s.

The trail described has short road walk sections but the rest is through dense woods with spectacular hills to climb, valley views, and walks along a wide, gurgling creek.

Bed & Breakfasts: Hanshaw House, 15 Sapsucker Woods Road, Ithaca, (607) 257-1437

Hound & Hare, 1031 Hanshaw Road, Ithaca, (607) 257-2821

Sweet Dreams B&B, 228 Wood Street, Ithaca (607) 272-7727

Boat Tour: Cayuga Lake Cruises, 704 W. Buffalo Street, Ithaca (800) 951-5901

Campgrounds: Buttermilk Falls State Park, Route 13, Ithaca, (607) 273-5761

Robert H. Treman State Park, Route 327, Ithaca, (607) 273-3440

Spruce Row, 2271 Kraft Road, Ithaca, (607) 387-9225

Outfitter: The Outdoor Store, 206 East State Street, Ithaca, (607) 273-3891

Trail Directions
• From the parking area, head west on the orange-blazed trail.
• Turn right (W) on a small gravel road.
• Pass a block pump house on the right.
• Turn right (SW) on Route 366. Follow Route 366 for 0.2 mile.
• Turn right (NW) on Freese Road. Follow Freese Road for 0.1 mile over the bridge.
• Turn left (W) onto a gravel farm road toward the sign "No Parking – Snow Plow Turnaround."
• The gravel road turns to a dirt lane along the edge of a field. Blazes are sporadic in this section.
• Continue straight and enter the woods. (You will not see the trail to the right. It is hidden behind brush.) The creek will be to your left.
• Reach the creek edge, then shortly meet the orange-blazed trail.
• Turn right (E) and head away from the creek. (Left heads to the suspension bridge over Fall Creek to Newman Arboretum.)
• Climb a steep hill.

244

- At 2.0 miles, reach a view of the valley to the left.
- Pass an unmarked trail from the left. Continue straight following orange blazes.
- At a "Y," bear right.
- Continue straight through a small trail intersection.
- At 2.4 miles, reach a "T." Turn left to stay on the Cayuga Trail. (Right heads down a steep hill to the field at the end of the gravel road taken earlier from Freese Road bridge.)
- Enter a field. Turn right and follow orange blazes along the edge of the field and woods.
- At 3.2 miles, turn right on the marked trail.
- At 3.3 miles, cross Freese Road.
- Walk along the back of a field containing a community garden. The cliff and creek are below on your right.
- Watch for the trail to turn right into the woods.
- The trail turns right, staying next to the gorge. (A side trail goes straight.)
- Pass a trail register at 3.7 miles.
- Exit the woods and turn right (E) along a field.
- Re-enter the woods and descend.
- At 3.9 miles, reach the bottom of the gorge and turn left (E).
- Climb out of the gorge.
- At 4.3 miles, exit the woods.
- Turn right, cross grass, and re-enter the woods in 100 yards.
- Pass a lookout over the creek.
- Reach a "Y" at 4.4 miles. Bear left, then cross an intersection.
- Cross a wide cinder trail. Quickly reach a "T" at the edge of a cliff and turn left. The creek will be on your right, far below.
- Walk steeply downhill, cross a seasonal streambed, then head uphill.
- A downhill, then cross a seasonal streambed.
- Reach the creek and bear left.
- Pass a trail to a house on the left.
- At 4.7 miles, reach Route 13. Turn right and cross on the bridge.
- Immediately after the bridge, turn right and head downhill across a field on a mowed strip, then into woods.
- Cross a small wooden bridge.
- At 4.8 miles, reach an abandoned railroad bed and turn right onto the wide mowed path.
- Pass a house on the left. Blazes are sporadic.
- At 4.9 miles, the orange-blazed trail turns right into the woods. The cliff to the creek will be on your right.

- Pass a trail register.
- Pass a trail to the right. Continue following orange blazes as the trail bends left.
- Cross a streambed.
- Cross a small wooden bridge and reach a "T."
- Turn left, pass the barricade, and reach the parking area.

Date Hiked: _____

Notes:

Definitions

Aqueduct: A stone, wood, or cement trough built to carry waters over an existing creek or river. The world's largest aqueduct for its time was built in Rochester to span the Genesee River. Eleven stone arches were erected, spanning 804 feet, to withstand the annual floods of this wild river.

Arboretum: A tree garden where a variety of trees are planted and labeled for study and enjoyment.

Bog: An acid-rich, wet, poorly drained, spongy area character-ized by plants such as sedges, heaths, and sphagnum.

Bushwhack: To make your way through a wild area without benefit of a trail to follow.

Carding: Combing of wool.

Corduroy: A method of spanning a wet section of trail by laying logs perpendicular to the trail. This creates a bumpy effect like corduroy material.

Deciduous: Describes trees that lose their leaves in winter.

Dike: An earthen bank constructed to hold water.

Drumlin: An elongated or oval hill created from glacial debris.

Esker: A ridge of debris formed when a river flowed under the glacier in an icy tunnel. Rocky material accumulated on the tunnel beds, and when the glacier melted, a ridge of rubble remained.

Feeder: A diverted stream, brook, or other water source used to maintain water level in the canal.

Fulling mill: A mill for cleaning wool and producing cloth.

Gristmill: A mill for grinding grain into flour.

Headrace: A trough or tunnel for conveying water to a point of industrial application.

Herbaceous: A seed-producing plant that does not develop persistent woody tissue but dies down at the end of a growing season.

Impoundments: Areas of marshland and ponds created by man-made earthen dikes.

Jewelweed: Also called touch-me-not, this plant is a member of the impatiens family. It grows in moist areas with a translucent stem and small snapdragon-like flowers in yellow, orange, or pink. The leaves shine silvery under water, hence the name jewelweed. The crushed plant has historically been used as a treatment for poison ivy, but recent studies show that it's not effective.

Lady's slipper: This perennial herb has a pouch-like flower that resembles a dainty slipper. A victim of habitat destruction and over-collection, this rare beauty is fast disappearing.

Leatherleaf: A shrub that grows on top of sphagnum moss and allows other plants to gain a foothold. It produces white, bell-like flowers in spring.

Marsh: An area of soft, wet land.

Mule: The sterile offspring of a male donkey and a female horse. Mules were often used to pull boats along the Erie Canal.

Purple loosestrife: An aggressive perennial imported from Europe, these blazing magenta flowering plants are spreading across American wetlands and crowding out native plants. The name derives from the early practice of placing this plant over the yoke of quarrelsome oxen. The plant was said to help the oxen "loose their strife" or quiet down.

Rebar: Round metal bars used to give structural strength (reinforcement) to cement.

Riparian zone: Land located on the bank of a natural waterway.

Sawmill: A mill for cutting trees into lumber.

Snag: Standing dead trees which provide dens and cavities for wildlife.

Sphagnum moss: A type of moss that grows in swamps and has an incredible capacity to hold water. It's estimated that this moss can can soak up over 100 times its own weight in water. In bogs where acids build up and oxygen is lacking, the moss compresses rather than degrades, and forms peat. Dried, shredded, and packed in bales, sphagnum moss is sold as peat moss and used by gardeners to retain moisture in soil.

Swamp: Wet, spongy land saturated and sometimes partially or intermittently covered with water.

Switchbacks: Winding the trail back and forth across the face of a steep area to make the incline more gradual.

Waste weir: A dam along the side of the canal which allows overflow water to dissipate into a side waterway.

Trails Under 2 Miles

Trails 2 to 4 Miles

Page	Trail Name	Length (miles)
90	Ontario Pathways – Phelps (round trip)	3.4
182	Bear Swamp State Forest – Short Loop	3.4
189	Fillmore Glen State Park	3.7
175	Howland Island	3.9

Trails 4 to 10 Miles

Page	Trail Name	Length (miles)
152	Texas Hollow State Forest	4.1
144&149	Watkins Glen & Queen Catherine Marsh	4.2
114	Hi Tor Wildlife Management Area	4.5
139	Goundry Hill State Forest	4.5
45&48	Genesee County Park – Inner & Outer Loops	4.7
120	Urbana State Forest – Short Loop	4.8
68	Rattlesnake Hill – Long Hike	5.0
101&104	Harriet Holister Spencer – Big Oak & Sidewinder Trails	5.2
162	Finger Lakes National Forest – Gorge Trail	5.4
156	Finger Lakes National Forest – Ravine Trail	5.7
85	Seneca Trail	5.8
110&114	Conklin Gully & Hi Tor Wildlife Management Area	6.5
242	Cayuga Trail	6.5
65&68	Rattlesnake Hill – Short & Long Hikes	7.0
51	Beaver Meadow Nature Center	7.0
124	Urbana State Forest – Long Loop	7.1
128	Keuka Lake Outlet Trail	7.5
186	Bear Swamp State Forest – Long Loop	7.8
204	Cayuga County Erie Canal Trail	9.3

Trails Over 10 Miles

Page	Trail Name	Length (miles)
208	Erie Canalway Trail	10.8
182&186	Bear Swamp State Forest – Long & Short Loops	11.2
156&162	Finger Lakes National Forest – Ravine & Gorge Trails	11.4
85	Seneca Trail (round trip)	11.6
128	Keuka Lake Outlet Trail (round trip)	15.0
204	Cayuga County Erie Canal Trail (round trip)	18.6
208	Erie Canalway Trail (round trip)	21.6
204&208&217	Cayuga County Erie Canal Trail & Erie Canalway Trail & Erie Canal Park	23.0

Contains a Wheelchair Accessible Trail

1 Boot Trails

2 Boot Trails

3 Boot Trails

3 Boot Trails

4 Boot Trails

Linear Trails

Loop Trails

Loop Trails

Trails to Waterfalls

Trails for Cross-Country Skiing

References

Finger Lakes Association
309 Lake Street
Penn Yan, N.Y. 14527
(800) KIT4FUN

Finger Lakes Interpretive Center
82 Seneca Street
P.O. Box 207
Geneva, N.Y. 14456
(315) 789-1431

The authors, Rich and Sue Freeman decided to make their living from what they love - hiking and bicycling. In 1996 they left corporate jobs to  spend six months hiking 2,200 miles on the Appalachian Trail from Georgia to Maine. That adventure deepened their love of the outdoors and inspired them to share this love by introducing others to the joys of hiking. Since most people don't have the option (let alone the desire) to undertake a six-month trek, they decided to focus on short hikes, near home. The result was *Take A Hike! Family Walks in the Rochester Area* which described hikes around Rochester, N.Y. In researching this book, the Freemans' got to more fully explore the wonderful Finger Lakes and Genesee Valley Region.

Rich and Sue have been active members of Victor Hiking Trails since its inception. They continue to do trail work and participate with other local trail groups as well. In addition, their passion for long distance hiking continues. In 1997 they thru-hiked the 500-mile long Bruce Trail in Ontario, Canada. Future hikes include a segment of the Florida Trail and traversing 500 miles of the Pacific Crest Trail through the state of Washington.

Since beginning their new career writing and publishing books, the Freeman's have pared down their living expenses and are enjoying a simpler lifestyle. They now have control of their own destiny and the freedom to head into the woods for a refreshing respite when the urge strikes. Still, their life is infinitely more cluttered than when they carried all their wordly needs on their backs for six months on the Appalachian Trail.

Other Books Available from Footprint Press

Take A Hike! Family Walks in the Rochester Area
ISBN# 0-9656974-60   U.S. $16.95   Can. $21.95
From parks to little known areas, this book describes 40 hikes within a 15 mile radius of Rochester, N.Y. Take the kids and dog along to explore the bounty of nature. Each trail has a map, description, and details you'll need such as where to park, estimated hiking time, and interesting things to see along the way.

Take Your Bike! Family Rides in the Rochester Area
ISBN# 0-9656974-28   U.S. $16.95   Can. $21.95
Converted railroad beds, paved bike paths, woods trails, and little used country roads combine to create the 30 safe bicycle adventures within an easy drive of Rochester, N.Y. No need to have a mountain bike – any sturdy bicycle will do.

Take Your Bike! Family Rides in the Finger Lakes & Genesee Valley Region
ISBN# 0-9656974-44   U.S. $16.95   Can. $21.95
Converted railroad beds, paved bike paths, woods trails, and little used country roads combine to create the 40 safe bicycle adventures through central and western N.Y. No need to have a mountain bike – any sturdy bicycle will do.

Bruce Trail – An Adventure Along the Niagara Escarpment
ISBN# 0-9656974-36   U.S. $16.95   Can. $21.95
Come along as experienced backpackers take you on a five-week journey along the Niagara Escarpment in Ontario, Canada. Explore the now abandoned Welland Canal routes, caves formed by crashing waves, ancient cedar forests, and white cobblestone beaches along azure Georgian Bay. Learn the secrets of long-distance backpackers. As an armchair traveler or in preparation for a hike of your own, you'll enjoy this ramble along a truly unique part of North America.

Alter – A Simple Path to Emotional Wellness
ISBN# 0-9656974-87   U.S. $16.95   Can. $21.95
Alter is a self-help manual which assists in recognizing and changing your emotional blocks and limiting belief systems. It uses easy-to-learn techniques of biofeedback to retrieve subliminal information and achieve personal transformation.

For sample maps and chapters explore our web site at:
http://www.footprintpress.com   263

Yes, I'd like to order Footprint Press Books:

\#

_____ *Take A Hike!* Family Walks in the Rochester Area

_____ *Take A Hike!* Family Walks in the Finger Lakes & Genesee Valley Region

_____ *Take Your Bike!* Family Rides in the Rochester Area

_____ *Take Your Bike!* Family Rides in the Finger Lakes & Genesee Valley Region

_____ *Bruce Trail* – An Adventure Along the Niagara Escarpment

_____ *Alter* – A Simple Path to Emotional Wellness

_____ Total Books @ $16.95 US or $21.95 Canadian each

For 1 or 2 books, add $3 per book for tax and shipping.
For 3 or more books, FREE (tax and shipping will be
    included in book price)

Total enclosed: $_____

Your Name: _____

Address: _____

City: _____ State (Province): _____

Zip (Postal Code): _____ Country: _____

Make check payable and mail to:
Footprint Press
P.O. Box 645
Fishers, N.Y. 14453

Or, check the web site at http://www.footprintpress.com

Footprint Press books are available at special discounts
when purchased in bulk for sales promotions,
premiums, or fund raising.